Danielle Wood and Marjorie Bligh at Marjorie's
Devonport home. (Photo by Bob Iddon)

DANIELLE WOOD

Housewife Superstar!

Danielle Wood is the author of a novel, *The Alphabet of Light and Dark* (2003; winner of The Australian/Vogel's and Dobbie literary awards), and a collection of stories, *Rosie Little's Cautionary Tales for Girls* (2006). She lives in Hobart and teaches at the University of Tasmania.

HOUSEWIFE SUPERSTAR!

Housewife Superstar!

Advice (and Much More) from a Nonagenarian Domestic Goddess

DANIELLE WOOD

ff

Faber and Faber, Inc.
An affiliate of Farrar, Straus and Giroux
New York

Faber and Faber, Inc.
An affiliate of Farrar, Straus and Giroux
18 West 18th Street, New York 10011

Library of Congress Cataloging-in-Publication Data
Wood, Danielle, 1972–
    Housewife superstar! : advice (and much more) from a nonagenarian
domestic goddess / Danielle Wood. — 1st American edition.
        pages   cm
    "First published by The Text Publishing Company 2011."
    Includes bibliographical references.
    ISBN 978-0-86547-889-3 (pbk. : alk. paper)
    1. Bligh, Marjorie, 1917–   2. Housewives—Australia—Tasmania—Biography.
3. Home economics.   I. Title.

DU195.3.B55 W66 2013
994.6'104092—dc23
[B]
                                                                    2012036562

Designed by W. H. Chong

www.fsgbooks.com
www.twitter.com/fsgbooks • www.facebook.com/fsgbooks

1   3   5   7   9   10   8   6   4   2

For my grandmothers,
Polly Hawkins and Barbara Wood

Time is the greatest gift there is. When time is gone, nothing else matters, so you must never waste it. You can't hoard it, like money—you can only spend it. But once it's spent, you can't get it back. You must spend it wisely, the first time—for it is the greatest gift you have.

Seasoning tip: Keep salt and pepper in one shaker for seasoning. Saves time. (3 of salt to 1 of pepper.)

—*Marjorie Bligh*

Contents

HOUSEWIFE SUPERSTAR!

Introduction

MADDEN Street, in the north-west Tasmanian town of Devonport, is a placid stretch of modest brick houses, obedient lawns, and lace curtains that you might fancy to be prone to the odd twitch. At number 163—a red-brick bungalow with a white weatherboard second-storey extension and a backyard graced by a scale replica of the Tamar River's Batman Bridge—lives housewife superstar Marjorie Bligh. As I write, she is ninety-four years old, and almost certainly muttering into her coffee cup about the dire consequences that will befall me if I fail to finish this book before she dies.

Domestic goddess and pioneer recycler, author and self-promoter, Marjorie is a formidable character. Thrice married, twice widowed and once divorced, she has produced a library of books, including a signature household manual revised and published under each of her married names. Her self-styled career as a newspaper columnist and author began in the 1950s, when she was squeezed out of competing in the domestic categories of Tasmania's regional agricultural shows after many years of mercilessly blitzing the competition with her jams, cakes, biscuits, bread, pickles, vegetables, flowers, knitting, sewing and crochet.

A queen of the household scene, Marjorie is the go-to girl when you have any manner of problem. She knows what to do when a goldfish has constipation (feed it Epsom salts), how to restore a crushed ping-pong ball (put it in boiling water), how to find the end of the sticky tape (hold it over a steaming kettle and wait for it to peel up) and what to do when you run out of rouge on your way to the ball (cut a beet in half and slap it on your cheeks). Raised in a time of privation, she knows how to unpick and lengthen the sleeves of children's sweaters, how to make mock oysters (it involves lambs' brains) and how to stretch butter from here to eternity. She knows that an old-fashioned corset-style brassiere can have a second life staked out in the garden as a plant protector and that you can glam up a pair of dull evening shoes with the addition of a pair of glittery clip-on earrings. Famous for never wasting a thing, Marjorie had her second-storey extension custom built as a museum to show off the items she has knitted and crocheted out of such unlikely materials as plastic shopping bags and used pantyhose. It also houses her handmade dancing gowns, souvenir teaspoons, toby jugs, scrap-books, and the bottle collection that was the pride and joy of her third husband, Eric Bligh.

For Marjorie, less is never more. In her home there is a place for everything, and everything is in its place—but there is scarcely an inch of surface space that has been left free of objects: ornaments, trinkets, photographs, certificates, pot plants, cushions, books, bric-a-brac. In her backyard there is no lawn, since every square foot of space is needed for garden beds in which to grow the hundreds of species of plants that she knows and loves.

Though grass-roots in her subject matter, Marjorie has always

*Marjorie Blackwell produces a batch of scones in the kitchen
at Climar, her iconic Campbell Town home.*

had her sights set on the stars. Her books feature forewords that
she has inveigled from such prominent Australians as Bob Hawke
and Dame Enid Lyons. Marjorie has sent sets of her books for the
edification of new prime ministers taking up residence at The Lodge,
as well as to presidents of the United States. In the forecourt of
Buckingham Palace she pressed a copy of one of her books into the
hands of Queen Elizabeth's private secretary.

The assessment of her biggest fan, Barry Humphries, is that
Marjorie is 'no slouch in the matrimonial department', either. During
her first marriage, to the jack of all trades Cliff Blackwell, Marjorie
had two sons and designed the family home that became the iconic
1950s Campbell Town property 'Climar' (the name is made up of the
first three letters of 'Cliff' and the first three letters of 'Marjorie').
Today the house is famed for its wedding-cake curves and a wrought-
iron fence studded with musical notes that sing out the opening bars
of the schmaltzy standard 'Melody of Love'. Marjorie's marriage to
Cliff was a sometimes violently unhappy one, and it sensationally

THINGS I LOVE
Composed by myself

I love the beautiful sunshine, the flowers and the dew,
But best of all in this wide world, I just love only you;
I love all kinds of music, new songs that are born each day,
Spring time with all its glory, and clothes that are bright and gay.
I love any kind of hobby, from knitting down to plastic;
I'm always making scrap books, I think they're so fantastic.
I love my roomy kitchen, with windows all around,
Where I can do my cooking with never ever a frown.
I love giving more than receiving—I hope you will agree,
And it's best to keep the golden rule and let your neighbours be.
I love the laughter of children ringing in my ears,
But few of us love the spoilt ones, they cause us too many tears.
I love both birds and animals, and of them I've quite a few;
I never get sick of sewing, or trying on something new.
In these verses I have written some of the things I love best,
But in the verses to follow are my hates, even down to my guest.

MY DISLIKES
—by me

I don't like morning visitors who never want to leave,
Or the ones who come with gossip—they really make me heave.
People who break promises, of that, I'll say no more,
Or the ones who say nothing, but yet they take the floor.
I just detest a windy day, doors creaking now and then,
Flies dirtying up the windows are worse than untidy men.
I don't like thoughtless people who enjoy making rows,
Or washing up a separator, or milking jolly cows.
Dusting is an awful job, I'd rather weed the garden;
I don't like working in good clothes, for all those who do, please pardon.
People late for appointments are really on the nose,
So are sockettes with high heel shoes and brightly painted toes.
Of people who think they're better than those just up the street,
They're the ones with their minds not occupied and the ones
    I don't want to meet.
I've finished all my hates and likes, or most of them we'll say,
But whatever goes on before me, I'm always thankful
    at the end of the day.

fell apart amid feverish small-town gossip about infidelity. One of Marjorie's sons has not communicated with her since she and his father divorced in the 1960s. Marjorie's second marriage, to the schoolteacher and former preacher Adrian Cooper, was punctuated with endless love notes, breakfasts in bed, and Marjorie's territorial sniping with Adrian's adult daughters. Following Adrian's death Marjorie met her third husband, Eric Bligh—a bus driver—while out and about on a CWA (Country Women's Association) excursion, snagging him with flirtatious glances in his rear-view mirror and promises of fruitcake.

It has not, however, been enough for Marjorie to live a life filled to overflowing with gardening, knitting, sewing, crochet, embroidery, husbands, pets, cakes and jam. She has also documented that life with discipline and zeal. Her daily diary has been kept religiously, as has a torrent of handwritten correspondence. Into a scrapbook go all her sentimental items, along with every newspaper and magazine article that strikes her as interesting. She donated 191 of her scrapbooks to the Tasmanian Archive and Heritage Office, but retains nearly as many at home.

Since the publication of her first book, in 1965, Marjorie has maintained a profile in the local press. But while many people know of her, they do not necessarily know much about her. Some refer to her as 'the one with all the husbands', before making glib intimations about suspicious circumstances in the cookery department. Others know her only as 'that woman who knits things out of old stockings'. But in addition to the knitted-up pantyhose and the three erstwhile husbands, there is another thing about Marjorie that continues to fascinate. And that is a rumour as enduring and dogged as the woman herself: a rumour so stubborn and hard to shift that not even Marjorie would be able to get it out of a white tablecloth with a mixture of methylated spirits, peroxide, lemon juice, cloudy ammonia and glycerine. This rumour has been so often repeated—in person, and in the Tasmanian press—that it has taken on the appearance of fact. Which is why many people will quite authoritatively tell you, when you mention Marjorie Pearsall/Blackwell/Cooper/Bligh, that she was the woman who inspired Barry Humphries' internationally celebrated housewife superstar, Dame Edna Everage.

<hr />

Though it was the Edna question that piqued my serious interest in Marjorie Bligh, I soon found myself intrigued by Marjorie herself. Within her masses of blunt prose is an extraordinary record of social, cultural and culinary change in Australia. While never at the vanguard of food trends, Marjorie and her recipes moved with the times. Inclusions and exclusions in each new edition of her household manual chart the evolving repertoire of ordinary Australian cooks. The emphasis on thrift in the first edition gives a powerful sense of how earlier generations provisioned their households on limited incomes, finding ways to replace expensive eggs in cake recipes, supplementing butter with cheaper ingredients to make it go further, and devising 'mock' ham, turkey and cream.

I also became interested in what Marjorie's life had to say about the circumstances and choices of women who lived through the twentieth century. I've heard it said that 'if Marjorie had put all that energy into politics, she would have been Australia's first female prime minister', and 'if Marjorie had put all that drive into being a doctor, she would have found a cure for cancer'. These backhanded compliments suggest that it has been a waste for her to spend her extraordinary energy and drive in the domestic sphere, on baking

I am self taught with everything, and have learned mostly by my mistakes.

Judging by your letters to me and verbal remarks, I think you think that I am a sort of freak, a dictionary or a doctor – someone who knows all the answers, but, my dear readers, I am only an ordinary person who has taught myself and learnt from my own and others' mistakes.

. . . the majority do not know the real Marjorie Bligh – the woman who has had to live in scanty clothes, with no father, little income, furnishings, amusement, playmates and strict discipline. In my younger days and beyond, there were never-ending demands on my time and energy, but I thought nothing of it. I have always observed that to succeed in the world one should seem a fool but be wise. My ambition was to try anything, and do everything well whatever the task, or whoever it was for. I never receive much appreciation ever, which to me is a great pity, for I think that better work would always be achieved if praise was more prevalent.

cakes, making dresses, starching tablecloths and removing stains—that energy and drive and intelligence ought to be spent in the public sphere, not the private, to be meaningful.

In recent years the Australian *60 Minutes* aired a segment titled 'Housewife Superstars', detailing a supposed trend for 'twenty-something Aussie mums' to return to the fixed gender roles of the 1950s. It was quintessential tabloid television: a handful of anecdotes construed into a social movement, a vague reference to a statistic that 'two-thirds of Australian women' would stay home if they could, a feisty cameo from Germaine Greer. The segment didn't convince me in the least, but it did draw my attention to the love-hate relationship

APRIL GIRL—ARIES

For all those born between March 21 and April 20
(My birthday is on the 14th April)
You are a leader born, and you will always Do or Die,
For you 'tis deeds, not words alone. Of work you are not shy.

Because all *Aries* have amazing energy, I am always a bit impatient with anyone who has not. I have a positive approach to life, am unpretentious and always in a hurry – striding instead of walking, and my whole attitude is one of openness and self-assurance.

my generation of women has with the domestic realm. While our grandmothers had Marjorie and others like her, we have Nigella Lawson, whose most famous book promises to teach us how to be a domestic goddess. Unlike Marjorie's books, though, Lawson's is addressed not to housewives but to working women with professional jobs who don't mind whipping up an impressive hazelnut torte on the weekend. A little extra accomplishment—not instead of, but in addition to, success in 'real' work. A frill, if you will. *How to Be a Domestic Goddess*, as Lawson says in her introduction, isn't about being a domestic goddess but about feeling like one, when the urge strikes. The book doesn't recommend that women return to the kitchen—only that it might be fun for them to holiday there.

Lawson is a success not only because she's a good cook and licks batter off her fingers in a decidedly come-hitherish way, but because she has capitalised on the trend for professional women to give themselves permission to indulge in domestic goddessery (on the weekends), provided they do it with tongue poked firmly in cheek. For the daughters of second-wave feminism, it's okay to knit

*Marjorie Blackwell demonstrates her
prize-winning cake presentation skills.*

and bake in the evenings after you've powered down your laptop. If you've got a profession securely in your pocket, you can spend your downtime in an apron without worrying that it's the thin edge of the anti-feminist wedge.

Amid this, Marjorie strikes me as an intriguing conundrum. She approached the job of housewife not without humour, but absolutely without irony. For her, professional housewifery is a serious and legitimate undertaking, unquestionably worthy of the highest levels of ambition. 'Being a housewife is a job, and I think I did a good job of it. I believed in starched tablecloths and serviettes. I even embroidered the tea towels. I was a happy little housewife,' she told me. This does not make her unusual among her generation, but Marjorie has never been content to be a domestic goddess only within her own home. Through her fiercely competitive approach to show cookery, and later through writing newspaper columns and books, Marjorie strove to make the domestic the wellspring of public recognition and success. While *60 Minutes* stressed the contentedness of those young women 'forsaking the corporate catfight' so they could spend their time cooking and cleaning, Marjorie's approach to housewifery had nothing to do with complacent contentment, or with retreat from the wider world.

While Marjorie wrote, published, distributed and signed each of her books with great seriousness, her work has not always been received in the same manner. She has one audience that treasures her works at face value—readers who refer to her recipes when they want to cook, and to her tips when they face a household problem. And she has another audience, one with more complex motives for reading and collecting her books. For this second group—which includes the current doyenne of sensible advice to Australian women, Kaz Cooke—Marjorie's works are a place to find history, fascination and amusement, as well as the odd useful recipe or handy home hint. For a time, a group of Hobart women hosted Marjorie parties, bringing dishes cooked from her recipes and wearing garments inspired by her patterns. Marjorie's poetry found unexpected accolades when some of her more memorable verses were performed, very loudly, by the Hobart Shouting Choir. And not so long ago a regular commenter

My books are in many parts of the world. People send them to friends, they show others, and it goes from there. The copy I took to Buckingham Palace in 1980 was welcomed so much, that the Queen's private secretary, Mr. William Heseltine, asked for one for his wife. In a letter to me Queen Elizabeth stated it was a "very useful and interesting volume". And from the White House in 1981, on a beautifully embossed card with their emblem, came this note of thanks from Nancy and Ronald Reagan, "We were delighted that you shared your original work with us. We look forward to enjoying it now and shall retain it for inclusion in our future Presidential collection. Please accept our sincere thanks for your thoughtfulness."

on 'A Pair of Ragged Claws', the blog of the *Australian* newspaper's literary editor, called Marjorie's autobiography 'the most inadvertently funny book I've ever read'. Clearly, Marjorie's works are ripe for comedic treatment, which makes it all the more tantalisingly plausible that she became a source of inspiration for the best known and most savage of Australian satirists, Barry Humphries.

In preparing this book I spoke with Marjorie, and with some of her friends and family members. I also contacted Barry Humphries' biographer Anne Pender, and his friend and colleague Brian Thomson, the theatre and film designer. And I finally got the chance to put the Edna question directly to Humphries himself. However, my primary sources have been textual. They include the various editions of Marjorie's six books, her newspaper columns, newspaper and magazine reports about her, and her scrapbooks and daily diary;

and Dame Edna Everage's works, including the autobiography *My
Gorgeous Life*, and the advice manuals *Dame Edna's Coffee Table Book:
A Guide to Gracious Living and the Finer Things of Life by One of the
First Ladies of World Theatre* and *Dame Edna's Bedside Companion*.

Marjorie's diaries prior to 1964 are no longer extant, but the
rest are now held by the Tasmanian Archive and Heritage Office.
When Marjorie prepared her autobiography, in 1986, she relied on
her memories of her years prior to 1964, and on her diary entries
from that year onwards. I too, therefore, find myself reliant on
Marjorie's memories of the first half of her life as presented in *Life
Is for Living: The Heartaches and Happiness of Marjorie Bligh: With
Snippets of Travel, Wisdom and History*; but in seeking to understand
her latter years I have had the benefit of the complementary sources
of the autobiography and the diaries. Without the narrative of the
autobiography, some of the diary entries would remain inexplicable.
Where the autobiography becomes evasive, the more forthright
diary entries often prove illuminating. Without a public audience in

mind Marjorie could write plainly in her diaries, whereas *Life Is for Living* attempts to shape the events of Marjorie's life for posterity in the public sphere. Part of her intention in writing the book was to defend herself against gossip and innuendo—the first line of her foreword is: 'I could not depart this life without writing my life story to put the record straight.'

In writing this book I sought not only to tell Marjorie's life story, and to investigate the Edna question, but also to compile the highlights of Marjorie's remarkable works. With Marjorie's generous permission, many of her recipes, hints and poems—along with a selection of her photographs—are reproduced verbatim in these pages.

G. W. Walkley, the one-time editor of Launceston's *Examiner* newspaper, was on the money when in a testimonial foreword to her 1965 cookbook he described Marjorie as 'an amazing collector and tester of recipes and household hints'. He went on to say that the book 'gives other housewives an opportunity to use many of the hints and recipes she has tried successfully'. Indeed, her books are, in the main, compilations of information gleaned from other sources; only the autobiography is primarily Marjorie's original work. In the introduction to *Crafts: Old—New—Recycled*, Marjorie writes: 'Thank God for friends and photocopying machines as I haven't had to do much writing with this book.' She states openly that the book purports only to share the 'beaut patterns that [she has] pasted in scrapbooks since childhood', but her bypassing of copyright concerns is still a touch astonishing.

Perhaps more than anything else, Marjorie is renowned simply for being herself: she has lived every chapter of her life passionately,

Marjorie's first book, the 1965 household manual Marjorie Blackwell at Home, *was created from scratch in the author's kitchen.*

ambitiously, tenaciously, eccentrically, publicly and with a compulsive desire to accomplish as much as possible. Her contributions to public life have been acknowledged in a swag of awards and honours. Closer to home, however, opinion is divided. While she is affectionately involved in the lives of her younger son, Ross, and most of her grandchildren, she remains estranged from her eldest son, Gerald. She has not had the affection of all of the stepchildren she acquired through her marriages to Adrian Cooper and Eric Bligh, though she has the devoted loyalty of some. She has been described as energetic, obsessive, generous, opinionated, forthright, hardworking, exacting, difficult, romantic, sentimental, warm, self-absorbed and hospitable. Certainly her personality is strong, and responses to it seem to be equally so.

With only a little education, but with a tremendous amount of determination, Marjorie forged a unique path towards public recognition. And although her duties as a homemaker circled around the needs of three husbands, I have little sense that her activities were ever controlled or even directed by these men. She was always driven by her own expectations of herself, holding herself to her own set of exacting standards, and I doubt that since the moment Marjorie first married she has ever been anything but her own fiercely independent mistress. She may have delightedly taken on a new name each time she got spliced, but she has never been anyone but her own incomparable self.

Marjorie, second from the right, is pictured with some of the important women in her life. Left to right: her mother, Emma; an aunt; her sister Beatrice; and her aunt Ruby.

Emma, Beatrice and Marjorie (right)
outside their cottage in Ross.

I

Marjorie Pearsall

MARJORIE Pearsall was born on April 14 of 1917, the same year that John F. Kennedy, Zsa Zsa Gabor, Vera Lynn and Ella Fitzgerald came into the world. In that year cinema screens were filled with Theda Bara's Cleopatra eyes and Charlie Chaplin's moustached face, and gramophones were spinning out popular wartime songs like 'Over There' and 'You're in the Army Now'. In the skies over Europe the Red Baron shot down twenty-one Allied planes in the month of Marjorie's birth. Though the conflict raging in Europe was far from her birthplace in rural Tasmania, two hundred miles from the southern coast of mainland Australia, Marjorie was not exempt from its impact. She was christened Marjorie Alfreda Willis Pearsall, her middle names a tribute to her uncles Alfred and William, who were away fighting on the battlefields of France. Of the two, only Alfred would return.

The township of Ross, where Marjorie was born, is a cluster of sandstone Georgian buildings on the edge of the Macquarie River, in the midst of the unprepossessing sheep country of the Tasmanian

Marjorie as a baby.

midlands. Today Highway 1 skirts the boundary of the historic township, and a short detour is required if you want to stop to hunt for antiques or admire the convict stonemasonry of Ross's famous bridge. But when Marjorie was born both the highway and the railway still bisected the town, and Ross was yet to become comfortably picturesque; in 1917 the town's past as a centre for the containment and deployment of convict labourers must not have seemed so distant. During Marjorie's childhood the town may have possessed a quiet beauty, but it's not hard to imagine the wide and sparsely populated streets as drab, particularly in the depths of a frosty winter.

Marjorie's parents lived on Waterloo Street, which still marks the eastern border of the neatly gridded town. Her father, Oscar William Pearsall, was the ploughman at the nearby property 'Bloomfield', where he had met her mother, Emma Beatrice Martin, when she was employed in the homestead as a domestic. Both Oscar and Emma had firmly colonial roots: among Oscar's forebears were settlers who arrived in the colony in 1804 with Lieutenant Governor David Collins' founding party, while Emma's grandfather Henry Nailer was a convict transported to Van Diemen's Land in 1844 for larceny.

Emma and Oscar tied the knot in St John's Church of England, Ross, in August 1910; and their employers, the Bennetts, bought for them the house on Waterloo Street, on the understanding that the Pearsalls would in time repay the debt. Made from locally quarried sandstone, the building had four rooms: two bedrooms, a 'front room' and a large kitchen. It was a neat house, with an iron-laced veranda and tidy picket fence fronting the street. Out the back was a four-acre allotment, bordered in turn by farmland plains and scrub. The young couple didn't have the luxury of a home to themselves: out of necessity, Emma's brothers Alfred and Harry shared the small dwelling. In 1912 the household increased by one with the birth of Oscar and Emma's first child, Doreen Elizabeth. Marjorie arrived five years later, followed in 1919 by Beatrice Ruby.

The first major event to shape Marjorie's childhood was the death of her father, in 1920. He died of tuberculosis in a Hobart hospital, leaving Emma to provide for her three girls—aged eight, three and

My mother was a gentle, loving, kind woman with good principles and believed in discipline. She encouraged me to write, collect, be thrifty, to sew, knit, crochet, cook, and to work in the home and garden, and to honour God. I do miss her greatly, as a mother is the best friend anyone can have. I cannot remember my father, I was too young, but Mother loved this little verse – "My house is small, no mansion for a millionaire, but there is room for love, and there is room for friends, that's all I care".

My Mother

A million lovely memories are what she left to me,
A bumper book of pictures which I flick through and see,
Her smiling face throughout the years, the twinkle in her eye,
The fun that we always had as years were passing by,
Every Sunday was a special day with church and Sunday School,
Inviting some one into tea, but, always The Golden Rule,
The dining-room all warm and cosy, and garden gay and bright –
The hours beneath the fruit trees, the shadow and sunlight,
Oh! It was fun, how proud I am that I had such a mother,
Who cared about her family and also her dear brother.

As children, we were not allowed to express our feelings to Mother or our teacher, we were not allowed to answer back even if we were in the right, and if we dropped a log of wood

one—on a small government allowance. She was also responsible for her brother Harry, who had a mild disability that was said to be the result of 'being dropped as a baby'.

Emma, strict and loving, firm and fragile, was now the dominant figure in Marjorie's life. She kept her girls primly dressed and socially on our foot, we couldn't say "damn", it was swearing. We had to be "seen and not heard", and were not to speak when grown-ups were speaking. How times have changed! We were not allowed to answer the door when there was a knock and sex was never mentioned, but today they say it is essential and we all know the results. When we were asked to do a job, we did it immediately. Now it is "Wait a minute". Discipline isn't practised these days. Children tell their parents what they want to eat, wear, where they want to go, and are allowed to sit up late at night. They answer the telephone when you ring the parents, which wastes time and money for the caller. Both parents in many cases have to work to cater for their children's expensive tastes, as they must have everything – from crazy looking bicycles to transistor radios. We received a present twice a year, but children today demand them anytime, and they frown if someone doesn't give them an expensive gift. Nothing given in these times is appreciated as children receive too much, too often. I've rarely been given expensive gifts, and anyhow I would rather earn my own, then there is no repercussion when there is an argument. Today there are several cars to the one home, in many homes the diet consists of take-aways, pies, pasties, Coke and from a tin, and sport seems to have replaced the learning of the three R's.

isolated, restricting them from playing with other children after school and on weekends. Emma was frugal, inclined to illness and resistant to change. She regarded her new electricity supply (connected in 1927, according to Marjorie) with suspicion, and during the only holiday she took in her life—all the way to Hobart, eighty-five miles away—she

Chest Cold (old remedy)

Moisten a square of brown paper in warm vinegar, sprinkle very thickly with black pepper, lay it on the chest, and bandage with flannel. Let it remain on several hours, as it will not raise a blister like mustard does.

Cough Stopper

My mother stopped our coughing at night, by roasting an onion before an open fire (leave skin on), turning it often. Then, with two forks, the centre was pulled out, topped with homemade butter and served.

Freckle Lotion

Equal parts honey, lemon juice and Eau de Cologne.

became miserably homesick. Marjorie's recollections paint her as elaborately superstitious, always on the lookout for omens of ill fortune:

New shoes weren't allowed on the table; the lid off the teapot brought visitors; spilling sugar was joy, salt was sorrow, unless you threw some over your left shoulder; if a picture fell off a wall, a relative was going to die, and it was bad luck to hang a picture over a doorway. Hanging a calendar before New Year's Day brought bad luck all year; walking under a ladder was bad luck; also passing someone on the stairs. Knives crossed, you were going to have an argument. The 13th, Friday and the colour green were also bad luck according to Mum. If she put a garment on inside out . . . she wouldn't turn it the right way out, it would stop there until she undressed at night; and if she was going out, and got a few yards away from the front gate, then realised she had forgotten something she wouldn't turn back to get it—bad luck if you did. Don't put up an umbrella or bring wattle in the house or it brings bad luck; so [does] transplanting parsley . . . You must put a cross on your shoe with spittle on your finger if you saw a white horse. Eating in the lavatory was feeding the devil, and if your left ear was burning someone was saying something bad about you, the right ear was something good. An itchy hand meant you were going to receive money and if you turned your money over when there was a new moon it would double the amount.

Emma claimed that a banging back gate was the harbinger of her husband's death. She said she heard the gate slam three times on the morning of the day he died in Hobart, but when she went outside to investigate no one was there.

Following Oscar's death the large garden at the rear of the Waterloo Street house became the key to the family's survival. It contained a vegetable patch and orchard, as well as accommodation for various animals. The produce from the garden was not only enough for the household's needs: there was a surplus that could be sold. Marjorie and her sisters worked hard. Their chores included picking and delivering buckets of fruit, and delivering butter as well as the rabbits, hares, kangaroos and wallabies that their Uncle Alf snared in the nearby bush. Wash day—an epic of bucket-carrying, boiling and scrubbing—was an all-day event.

The kitchen of the Waterloo Street home was the centre of activity.

Bleeding Cuts
Olden day method was to stop it bleeding with some white pepper put in cut.

Croup (old recipe)
One dessertspoonful methylated spirit, two dessertspoonfuls of vinegar, three dessertspoonfuls water. Saturate a strip of flannel in this and wrap around the throat, covering with a dry strip. Gives instant relief; or,
Wrap the child in a blanket, hold to a closed window, then throw the window up suddenly, and the spasm will be relieved; or, take the child, well wrapped up, for a car ride. Hold its head to a half open window and allow the night air to rush past its face (Dr R. M. Webster's cure), or,
Put feet in a bag of cut-up onions, tie around the ankles and leave on feet all night in bed.

Pimples

Mix 3 tablespoons treacle with 2 teaspoons sulphur and take 1 teaspoon after each meal.

Sore (that won't heal)

Get some young blue gum leaves, dip them in boiling water. When leaves are limp, put as hot as possible on the sore, wrap it up and when the leaves are dry, put another lot on. It heals in no time.

Warts Cure

Put banana skin on them, white side down, and leave for several days, or until they go away; or,

Warts disappear in 3 months if you rub them with castor oil before going to bed, or daub them with kerosene every day, or with a slice of garlic, or with 1 tablespoon of bicarbonate of soda dissolved in 2 tablespoons of water. Another hint is to melt a small piece of washing soda in vinegar and daub warts several times a day. I had them as a child and my mother told me to lick them on awakening and one morning they weren't there.

Diphtheria

Light sulphur and let patient inhale the fumes. The fungus will shrink and die. Taken from a very old reliable book.

Here, a pine-topped table served for dining, ironing, mixing cakes, cutting out frocks, washing up; and for Emma's assorted industries, including making jams, pickles, sauces, candles, bread, butter. The white flagstones of the kitchen floor were cleaned with pipeclay, and the pine dresser, kitchen table and toilet seat scrubbed with sandsoap. The silver, pots and pans were cleaned with ashes, and knives were cleaned by pushing their blades into the earth in the garden. Emma, Doreen and Marjorie spent evenings industriously: sewing clothes by hand, knitting stockings and embroidering.

Marjorie writes that 'there were no luxuries in our house', yet this is not exactly true. In Emma's household, the girls had all the basics as well as the means for the occasional treat. There were gifts for birthdays and at Christmas, although rarely at other times, and sweets were allowed on Fridays. Not all chores were unpaid—if the girls did a good day's weeding or sowing, they were rewarded with sixpence to spend on cheesecakes or Chelsea buns at the bakery.

Sunday school and services at St John's punctuated the family's week, and the Sunday school anniversary and annual picnic marked out their year. Emma and her girls also attended anniversaries and special services at the local Methodist church, so 'church, church and more church' constituted the Pearsalls' limited social life. Marjorie and her sisters each received a new dress (sewn by the local dressmaker) on the Sunday school anniversary, whereupon the old dress was let down and worn to school.

School in Marjorie's time was writing on slates, chanting times tables and reciting the alphabet, backwards as well as forwards. For the girls there was also knitting, crocheting and learning to use a treadle sewing machine. Marjorie was eager to please, and she would take apples, pears and other fruits to school for her adored teacher, Miss Johnson. Little Marjorie was heartbroken when Miss Johnson rebuffed her bounty, telling her not to bring any more fruit—the cupboard was full.

While Marjorie's family sometimes struggled to make ends meet, others in the

> **KEROSENE SOAP No. 1**
> **7 lbs. salt-free fat, 7 quarts water, 1 lb. caustic soda, ½ lb. resin, 2 small packets Lux, 2 small packets of washing powder, 2 tablespoons borax, ½ cup kerosene.**
> Put all ingredients into a kerosene tin, except kerosene, and bring to the boil, taking care it does not boil over. Stir until thick (about 1 hour). Add kerosene about 10 minutes before taking off fire. It will boil up quickly when kerosene is added, so be careful and stir well.

district suffered acute poverty. Marjorie recalls children walking quite a distance to school without shoes or boots, and another child who didn't have bloomers to wear under her school dress. Door-to-door beggars were part of the social fabric and, although the Pearsalls received their own charity from the landed gentry (after Oscar's death, food and clothing parcels came from the Bennetts of Bloomfield), Emma felt it was her station to give to the less fortunate. When one beggar came to the door asking for food, Emma told him she had nothing but the meat cooking in her pot. He said that would do, and she protested that she had nothing to wrap it in. That didn't matter, he said, so she hooked the meat out with a carving fork and brought it to the door. He opened his flannel shirt and tucked the scalding-hot meat inside it against his skin, and went on his way.

A local man, Micky Clark, became something of a regular charity case at the Pearsall household. He had been living with his sister Sarah but, after she died, he began calling in to Emma's for afternoon tea, then for tea. After a time he became bolder still, and would ask for soap and a towel on his arrival. Marjorie writes: 'we found out that he had no money for food, wood or soap, because, besides drinking, he gave it to a priest to get Sarah out of Purgatory. At one stage he told Mum [that Sarah's] legs were out, another time her arms, and so it went on.'

On one occasion Micky arrived to find Marjorie sitting on the front step knitting. She said that her mother wasn't home, but he pushed past her into the house. In a rush of spite, Marjorie stood up and trod on a piece of rag that was jutting out of a hole in Micky's boot—he had rags wound around his feet in place of socks—making him fall over. For that, she later got a thrashing and was sent to bed.

As well as beggars there were hawkers—although the distinction

Opposite – my great grandmother
            Emma Tailer.
Top left – my maternal grandmother,
        below Eliza Martin.
Top right and bottom left – her husband
my grandfather, William Walter Martin
outside the family home he built for $100.
Their family left to right – Harry Charles,
Emma Beatrice, Maud Elizabeth, sitting
Ruby, Mary Eliza. Two Sons Alf and Bill
were at the war ★.   Taken at Ross.

more Martin photos on inside back cover

Marjorie's maternal grandfather, William Martin, abandoned his wife, Eliza, and their six children
(four are pictured here, including Marjorie's mother) to begin a new family with his wife's younger sister.

was not always clear. One of the more colourful characters was Mrs 'One-eye' Brown, who had 'one eye and a hole where the other one should have been'. She came with a cart piled high with wares, and a mangy horse and several dogs. As well as selling her goods, which included handmade willow clothes pegs, she would beg meat for her dogs, gather firewood in backyards and request old clothing. If given a hat, she would put it on top of the one she was wearing. According to Marjorie, Mrs Brown was bad-tempered when crossed, and once threw a bucket of water over the butcher when he refused her free meat. She also gave Marjorie and her younger sister, Beatrice, a pair of hearty smacks across the face when she caught them peeping at her through a shop window. Mrs Brown would approach houses loudly singing 'My Blue Heaven', and Emma would gather her daughters inside and lock the door when she heard her coming. Mrs Brown 'knocked at the door; no answer, so she banged hard and sang out, "I know you're in there, Mother Pearsall, so now I'll let your kangaroo rat out!" and she did just that, and my goodness, it was hard to catch again.'

It was rumoured that Mrs 'One-eye' Brown was in fact a wealthy woman from Hobart who dressed as a tramp to go out profiteering. Whether or not this unlikely story was true, she remained a character in the midlands for some time, and turned up peddling her wares at Marjorie's own door after Marjorie was married.

MOCK TURKEY SPREAD

3 tomatoes, 2 tablespoons butter, 4 tablespoons grated cheese, 4 tablespoons fine white breadcrumbs, ½ small onion (finely grated), 1 egg, pepper and salt to season, pinch herbs.

Peel tomatoes and cut roughly. Melt butter, add tomatoes, seasoning and onion. When tender, mash smoothly and add beaten egg. Stir until thick. Remove from heat and add cheese and crumbs. Put in small airtight jars.

The young Marjorie Pearsall was a brown-haired, blue-eyed girl of average height, average weight, average looks. While strong, she was not athletic, having—as she put it—'no wind for running'. She was no saint, but when she was naughty it was usually only in a common or garden-variety way: carelessly leaving a precious doll out in the rain, getting out a treasured balloon against orders and bursting it, or taking advantage of a lenient aunt who came to take care of her and her sisters while their mother was sick.

Among Marjorie's signature traits to emerge in childhood were her industriousness and determination. When still at school she made extra money for the household by running errands for her teachers and by cleaning the schoolrooms during holidays. As soon as she could knit and sew she was selling her skills. At one point she was paid to knit red, white and blue sweaters for the local football team—and hand-knitting eighteen identical sweaters is no mean feat. She had 'stickability', being able to finish long and sometimes tedious projects that others would give up on. She also learned to be a perfectionist, undoing projects and beginning again if they had any flaws. Out of necessity, Marjorie was a very capable child. When Emma was unwell and admitted to hospital in nearby Campbell Town, her unmarried sister Ruby would usually take time off from her job in Launceston and travel to

> **DEVILLED TRIPE**
>
> Cut 1 lb. tripe in small pieces, roll in flour and fry in hot fat. Pour off all but 1 tablespoon fat, and make a brown gravy with it. Put in a saucepan, add 1 sliced onion, 1 large tomato, pepper and salt. Simmer 20 minutes. Serve hot on toast with mashed potato.

AUSTERITY PUDDING

Rub 1 tablespoon butter into 1½ cups of sifted S.R. flour and mix to a light dough with ½ cup milk to which has been added 2 tablespoons boiling water. Put dough in basin (not greased) and pour over the following mixture: ½ cup sugar, 1 tablespoon golden syrup or honey, 2 dessertspoons butter, ½ cup boiling water. Do not put a lid on the basin, only put lid on the saucepan when steaming. Delicious and cheap.

SISTER BEATRICE'S BISCUIT CAKE

½ lb. icing sugar, 2 level dessertspoons cocoa, 1 teaspoon vanilla essence, 5 ozs. melted solid white shortening (not hot), 2 tablespoons milk, coffee biscuits, softened by exposure.

Line a square tin with greaseproof paper. Mix dry ingredients in a bowl. Stir in melted copha [white shortening] and milk. Fill tin with alternative layers of mixture and biscuits and allow to set. Ice with chocolate icing.

P.S. – 1 teaspoon coffee essence added to melted shortening makes a delightful change.

SISTER DOREEN'S HONEY CAKES

Will keep a long time, wonderfully moist until the last.
6 ozs. butter and 6 ozs. sugar, 1 tablespoon honey, 3 eggs, 8 ozs. flour, 1 teaspoon baking powder, pinch salt.

Cream butter and sugar, add honey, then eggs, one at a time with a tablespoon of flour with each addition. Sift the remaining flour with rising and salt and fold in last. Bake in patty tins a dessertspoon of the mixture for 15–20 minutes in hot oven. When cold, ice with honey icing.

Ross to look after her nieces. But once, when Ruby could not cover for Emma's absence, Marjorie and Beatrice looked after themselves. As there was no money they survived by eating pumpkin (roasted, baked in bread, cooked in soup) at every meal, for days.

An interest in ailments and their cure began in Marjorie's childhood. While she didn't relish her illnesses, she enjoyed the rare opportunity to escape daily chores and bask in her mother's loving attention. She recalls her minor childhood afflictions and treatments with clarity, remembering how Emma would ward off colds by putting an unpeeled onion in front of the fire, turning it until it was cooked, then pulling out the centre, dotting it with butter and giving it to the girls to eat. She also insisted that they drink olive oil to prevent illness. Still, Marjorie suffered from bronchitis during several winters of her childhood, and developed a taste for the medicines she was given: Scott's Emulsion and Hearn's Bronchitis Cure. Because of Marjorie's constant coughing, her bed was moved from the shared bedroom to the front room, where she slept all night with a fire burning and a candle lit. The attending doctor advised Emma to put Marjorie into flannel and not remove it until the bronchitis was cured, so Emma bought baby flannel and fashioned singlets with crocheting around the neck and sleeves—to this, Marjorie attributes her return to good health.

Marjorie's tendency to walk on the sides of her feet also became a cause for medical attention. A doctor recommended that she wear boots to strengthen her ankles, but fashion-conscious Marjorie kicked up a fuss and threw a pair of new boots down the passageway in disgust. Emma solved the sartorial problem by adapting heavy knitted stockings that could be worn over the tops of the boots, like gaiters. She also massaged Marjorie's feet with warmed olive oil and encouraged Marjorie to walk around the house with marbles under her toes, and these measures, Marjorie writes, solved the problem.

Marjorie was the daughter of the household who took most to heart her mother's 'waste not, want not' credo. This emphasis on thrift, combined with an intrinsic sentimentality, meant that Marjorie kept—and continues to keep—just about everything she ever acquired. It's not, perhaps, so surprising that in her nineties she still has little trinkets like the letter M brooch that her mother bought for her from a door-to-door hawker. It is remarkable, though, that as a child she thought to keep the slip of paper her mother wrapped the gift in and wrote on, and that she has kept it all her life.

Marjorie's childhood and young womanhood permitted few glimpses of frivolity, but when they did come it was usually courtesy of her aunts—her mother's sister Ruby, and her Uncle Alf's wife, Amy. When Ruby came to stay she would bring glittering evening frocks, bags, jewellery and shoes, and model them for her nieces while waltzing, solo, to gramophone records. She must have cut quite a dashing figure with her waist-length curly hair, singing along with her records in her strong soprano voice. Aunt Amy, whom Alf had brought over from England after the war, came to regional Tasmania with a range of accomplishments. As well as being a skilled dressmaker she could compose music, play the organ, play tennis and recite poetry. Music lessons and other entertainments were out of the question for Marjorie, who was usually occupied with chores, so

Marjorie's parents, Emma Martin and Oscar Pearsall, on their wedding day in August 1910.

beautiful clothes, music and dancing all became markers of an adult life to which she aspired. Her chief recollection of being confirmed in the Church of England was of 'feeling like a queen' in her new white dress, veil and stockings. Her first experience of silk stockings and garters came at age fourteen, when she wore them to church and 'strutted about like a peacock, showing them off'.

As she grew, Marjorie was prevented from having any extended contact with boys, and was kept remarkably ignorant about matters of sex and reproduction. She reports that she learned about pregnancy from a lad called Ernest, the visiting grandson of a neighbour.

> Once when Ernest came alone, I asked him where his mother was and he replied 'She's going to have a baby.' I asked him what he meant, and he told me. I told him not to be so filthy, and he replied it was a fact, but I still could not digest it, or even want to believe it. It was ridiculous. No way could a baby get in, or out, of your body, I told myself. I was confused, but never asked mother if it was true. After I was told that, I watched married women very closely and yes, they became fat and slim again . . . All Mum told me when I first menstruated was that it would occur every month, what to use and when, and I had to put my feet up when I came home from school until I went to bed. I wasn't to wash my head or have a bath, and not to tell Beatrice.

It seems extraordinary that a girl surrounded by pets and livestock of all kinds could remain so sheltered from the facts—hard to credit that she would not, prior to Ernest's revelation, have witnessed animals mating, gestating or giving birth. There was, though, a good deal of primness surrounding the household's animal population. Marjorie and her sisters were not to call a ram a ram: it was a 'father sheep'. A bull was a 'gentleman cow' and a bitch was a 'mother dog'. The words 'drake' and 'rooster', however, were not considered inappropriate. Marjorie writes that she and her sisters didn't know why their cows were taken to visit a local farmer's bull, and that, when questioned,

> ## MRS BEETON'S MARMALADE
> **4 large Seville oranges, 3 lemons, 7 pints water, 7 lb. sugar.**
>   Cut up oranges and lemons. Squeeze juice and put in separate basin.
> Save pips. Slice fruit, peel thinly (on a china plate to preserve natural
> oil) and place in basin. Cover fruit peel with 7 pints of water and allow
> to stand for 24 hours. Cover pips with water. Bring rind and water (in
> which it has been soaking) to the boil, and simmer gently for about
> an hour. Pour back into basin and leave for 12 hours. Put fruit juice,
> water off pips, and rind and water into a saucepan, add sugar, and stir
> until sugar is dissolved. Boil rapidly until it will set (about 30 minutes).
> Makes about 10 jars.

Emma 'always made up some story'. Again, it seems strange that Marjorie didn't observe the cows, on their return, growing larger or giving birth.

This obfuscation of sexuality could not prevent the girls from eventually making their own discoveries. One morning in 1930, when Marjorie was thirteen, her mother went to rouse eighteen-year-old Doreen, only to find that the bed was empty and had not been slept in. Emma Pearsall was distraught, almost hysterical; she soon learned that Doreen had left with Charles Cook, aged fifty-one, whom many locals had thought was courting Emma herself. Cook had been paying Emma to do his washing and ironing, and would stay a while to chat when he came to collect it. Often she would walk halfway home with him. Apparently, writes Marjorie, 'after Mum left him at night and came back home, he would double back and see Doreen.' The household, Marjorie says, 'never recovered from [the] shock' of Doreen's eloping.

Some years later, Marjorie was weeding in the front garden when a car pulled up outside the house. From it emerged Doreen and her two sons, George and Lovell, aged about three and one, immaculately dressed in black velvet breeches with silk shirts, white socks and black patent leather shoes. Doreen had brought gifts for the family, including a china tea set for her mother and patent leather bags for Marjorie and Beatrice (Marjorie still has hers). 'I don't think I would be exaggerating,' Marjorie writes, 'if I said that that afternoon was the happiest time in my life. We loved and missed our sister very much.' Doreen divorced Cook and remarried, this time staying in contact with her mother and sisters.

Though Emma could not shelter her younger daughters from the Doreen affair, she did for a long time manage to keep them ignorant of another family scandal playing out before their eyes. Throughout her childhood, Marjorie writes, she believed she had no maternal grandfather. She had no idea that this grandfather was actually living in Bridge Street, about half a mile away from the cottage in Waterloo Street, with his second family. Marjorie's grandfather William Walter Martin married her grandmother Eliza in 1887. Between 1888 and 1899 the couple had six children, of whom Marjorie's mother was the eldest. Eliza had a younger sister, rather unimaginatively named Elizabeth, and in about 1907 William Martin brought her to live with his family in Ross. The following year Elizabeth gave birth to his son Geoffrey. This explosive event broke up the first family: Eliza went to work at the property Bloomfield, where Emma was by this time already working, and the children still needing care were entrusted to various relatives. William and his second wife, Elizabeth, had a further six children, the youngest born in 1920. Marjorie must have gone to school with her step-aunts and step-uncles, not knowing how closely they were related.

When I imagine Marjorie as Miss Pearsall, I like to think of her on her fourteenth birthday—April 14, 1931—the day she was expected to finish school. Unlike most of her classmates, who were champing at the bit to leave their schooldays behind, Marjorie loved the order and calm of the classroom, even though she did not do especially well in her exams.

> I even had to sit for my final exam twice, but failed the second time too. I was always alright until the day of the examination, then my mind would go blank and my eyes would only see the minister at the table . . .
> All I could do was watch that clock, once the papers were handed out, instead of concentrating on the questions. I became so tense I felt half unconscious. Each time I did exams, Mum said that if I passed she would buy me a watch, so I did try as I really wanted that watch. Strangely enough though, next day, the same questions I answered with ease if I sat alone with them on the veranda . . . All I ever scored for my exams were 47 marks, but 50 was required to pass.

Marjorie begged to be allowed to stay at school until the Christmas break. She gained eight months' more education, but when the summer came her future looked much the same. She was a young woman with little money and an average education. 'Options? Well, we just didn't really have very many options in those days,' she told me. 'I dreamed of being an actress, flitting about in pretty clothes I'd make myself. For a while there, I thought about being a nurse. I thought it would be nice to look after people, but seeing my mother in hospital turned me off that idea.'

Once she left school Marjorie didn't go looking for work—it regularly came looking for her. First, a local family whose cook was on long service leave asked Emma's permission to employ Marjorie for the period of her absence. Marjorie was delighted with the opportunity, not only because she would be able to try out her

Marjorie (centre) with her elder sister, Doreen, and younger sister, Beatrice.

skills in a new setting, but also because it was a chance to broaden her horizons, meet new people and observe the lifestyle of a more prosperous family.

Word of Marjorie's abilities must have spread, and soon the mistress of the Campbell Town property Rosedale applied to Emma for Marjorie's services. Young Marjorie was impressed by the colonial homestead, by its rosewood and mahogany furnishings, and in her recollections she notes the solid cedar shutters on the windows, originally installed to repel 'aborigines or bushrangers

Butter: To make it go further, put into a small saucepan, 2 heaped teaspoons of full cream powdered milk. Add 1 teaspoon powdered gelatine and ½ teaspoon of salt. Mix in gradually ½ cup milk, and stir over fire until hot, but not boiling. Cool a little and cut into this ½ lb. of butter. Stir and blend with a wooden spoon and put into a basin. Twice as much butter and more nourishing.

If you haven't any scales, an easy way to cut a ½ lb. of butter if required, is to cut through the pound diagonally and you will be sure of an accurate measure. Another easy way for measuring ½ cup butter (or ¼ lb.) without scales is to fill a cup half full of water and drop butter in until the cup is full or reaches the top. Drain butter before using.

"Wonder butter" for use at kitchen teas, balls, etc., in sandwiches can be made by putting 1 lb. cut up, soft butter in a bowl and add a teaspoon of salt and gradually add 1 cup hot water and 1 cup cold water alternately until all used. Beat well with beater when all is absorbed. Goes twice as far.

If uncovered butter has absorbed other food flavours in the refrigerator, cut it into small pieces, cover with fresh milk and leave for an hour. Strain off milk and the butter should be sweet again.

Buy a butter curler and fill up your butter dishes with curls. Takes only a few minutes, but will save up to ¼ lb. of butter a week, as it is easier to spread and saves putting it on bread in big blobs when children are around.

Home-made Furniture Polish: An old, but trustworthy polish for furniture easily made at home is as follows: mix together 1 gill of turpentine, 1 gill of linseed oil, ½ gill of methylated spirits, and ½ gill of vinegar. Shake well before use. Use sparingly with a soft cloth. A gill is 7 tablespoons.

Parcels: Before tying parcels to be sent by mail, wet the string. This not only makes the knot easier to tie, but as the string dries, it shrinks and makes the parcel more firm.

[outlaws]'. This time the job involved cooking, cleaning, and minding a young girl whom Marjorie regarded as spoilt and uncontrollable. At first, vacuuming and dusting the beautiful and barely used upstairs rooms was a pleasure to Marjorie, but she eventually tired of cleaning already clean rooms, so she developed a habit of putting on the vacuum cleaner and sitting down to knit for half an hour. Perhaps the mistress of Rosedale twigged to this ruse, or perhaps she and Marjorie were simply not well matched. In any case, prior to leaving for a holiday in Melbourne, the lady of the house sacked Marjorie—apparently because Marjorie didn't sound her aitches properly and the lady didn't want her daughter to grow up speaking in such a common fashion. Marjorie, terrified of facing her mother with the news that she'd been fired, took a friend home with her to soften the blow.

The next woman to come to Emma's door to employ Marjorie was Mrs Crosby Lyne of Riccarton, a property located just east of Campbell Town, and her offer set Marjorie's adult life on its course. Marjorie didn't agree with some of the practices of the household, such as scraping soured cream out of sponge cakes and refilling them with jam for the workmen to eat, or being instructed to call the children of the house 'Miss' and 'Master'.

> That will be the day, I said to myself, when I'll call a three year old 'Miss', and I never gave any of them those titles in all the time I was there. The first few months I often found a sixpence or a shilling under place mats, vases, etc., put there to test my honesty, but they soon tired of that.

After a time Marjorie found Mrs Lyne to be a kind and compatible employer. Marjorie's wages were one pound a week, and with this princely sum she first bought a wireless radio for her mother, then a pair of plush doormats for her mother's hall. After that, it was a

Broad Beans – Put a bunch of parsley in with broad beans when cooking them, and they will not turn black and the flavour will also be improved.

winter coat for herself, with a large grey fur collar that made her feel incredibly glamorous. It was Mrs Lyne who first encouraged Marjorie to enter some of her homemade goods in the Campbell Town Show, sparking an interest that would become a near obsession for the young cook. Her first entry was a pound of butter, for which she won first prize: the blue ticket, and two shillings and sixpence. Most likely, it was the recognition rather than the financial reward that spurred Marjorie to enter in more categories at more shows as the years went on.

It was at Riccarton that Marjorie met her future husband Cliff Blackwell, the lad in charge of caring for the property's horses. From photographs, and reading between the lines of Marjorie's somewhat jaundiced descriptions, Cliff was a towheaded country boy, somewhat rough around the edges. He was one of ten children born to a gruff father and a long-suffering mother, and he seems to have been content enough with his lot in life. Cliff's and Marjorie's aspirations were perhaps never in accord, and nor did their romance get off to an auspicious start.

One night he asked me if I would like to go to a dance at [the nearby town of] Conara the next Saturday night and I accepted. He took me on the back of his motorbike. He couldn't dance, and I only a little, so we sat there like dopes until a lad named George (Bluey) Ashman asked me to get up in a waltz. I did, and he patiently taught me a few more steps, then kept coming back and back, and as he was handsome, I didn't mind. In spite of all this, when I returned to my seat after the last dance, Cliff was gone, so Bluey said he'd take me home on the handlebars of his bicycle. I didn't fancy trying to sit on handlebars for nine miles but I had no choice, so gathering up my frock, I clambered on, and away we went in the cold frosty night. When we were about halfway home we came upon a man whose vehicle had broken down on the side of the road. We stopped to see who it was and behold it was Cliff, so Bluey just pedalled on. It's not printable what Cliff said to us, but we laughed all the way home.

Cliff 'soon got over it' and, once the relationship became more serious, he and Marjorie became co-owners of an Australian terrier pup that they named Shandy Gaf. The young couple idolised the dog, Marjorie ferrying him around in a basket on the front of her bicycle.

By the time Marjorie was twenty she had settled on Cliff as a husband, and all her energy was going into preparing to become the mistress of her own home. This was a task she approached with excitement, and with her characteristic tenacity and drive. The betrothed couple bought a home on the main street of Campbell Town, which they renovated by candlelight. They would cycle to the house after tea at Riccarton, work until midnight, then return to sleep. Marjorie spent her spare minutes planning and listing, and poring over catalogues from Myer in Melbourne, and went without new clothes and holidays so that she could buy goods for her future home. She waited eagerly for the courier, who would come in his truck with parcels from Melbourne, the contents of which cluttered her small room at Riccarton. While she bought all the household items, such as linen, cutlery and crockery, Cliff—on his higher salary of one pound and ten shillings—bought or made their furniture. The weatherboard home in Campbell Town had a staircase with a corner at the landing, so parts of walls had to be dismantled for furniture to be hauled into the upstairs bedrooms.

It's not difficult to imagine Marjorie

Possums in the Ceiling
Put some flowers of sulphur in a foil dish in the ceiling and set it alight, and you won't be troubled again.

concentrating more passionately on the business of nest making than on the business of scrutinising her future partner.

> I was eager to get married, as I was sick of being told what to do. Cliff was my only boyfriend, as we weren't allowed boys, so to me he was a blessing in disguise whatever his faults. I was house-happy and wanted to be a housewife, as I was brimming over with ideas and bursting to put them into practice.

Marjorie's naivety, and that of her sister Beatrice, would soon have serious consequences. In the winter of 1937 twenty-year-old Marjorie was scrubbing the floor at Riccarton when a phone call came for her, telling her that her mother was seriously ill. Emma was coughing up blood—like her husband before her, she may have had tuberculosis. She was hospitalised in Campbell Town and died a week later, leaving Marjorie and Beatrice orphaned and devastated. Uncles and aunts rallied to comfort the girls, to help with the funeral arrangements and make decisions about what to do with the family home and its contents. Aunt Ruby at this time had a paramour, George, whom she had agreed to marry—Marjorie writes—on the understanding that there was to be 'no sex life'. (Having seen one of her sisters in labour, Ruby was terrified of giving birth.) George was present the day after Emma's funeral when Marjorie and Beatrice decided to unlock their mother's sideboard. There they discovered calico bags full of valuables, including silver, and stacks of one-pound notes. George volunteered to take the money and valuables to a safe place to count up their value and, trustingly, the girls allowed him to do so. They also let him take their money in a suitcase to Launceston—where, he said, he would open bank accounts

Mice
Push steel wool, not paper, into their hole (not the soap-impregnated kind). They cannot chew steel wool.

Marjorie in her late teens.

for them. Marjorie later wrote to George asking for her money, but it was never seen again. Ruby became the victim of a similar scam, so she never entered into her chaste marriage contract. After Emma's death the house on Waterloo Street had tenants for a time, but it was later abandoned, then condemned. To Marjorie's great sadness, it was eventually demolished.

On April 14, 1938, Marjorie Pearsall turned twenty-one. In the absence of parents to do the honours, Aunt Amy stepped in to organise a birthday party at the Ross Sunday School, and Marjorie

WATTLE BIRDS

Brush each bird over with warmed butter after plucking them. (Do not clean birds in any other way; their insides are left intact). Tie a thin slice of fat bacon over each breast. Put in a fry pan (electric) on a wire grid and cook slowly for 5 or 6 hours. Take off wire grid after 3 to 4 hours, and cook in the fat that has dripped off them. Baste often. Serve on buttered toast.

MUTTON BIRD STUFFED RABBIT

Soak mutton bird overnight in boiling water in which has been dissolved a piece of washing soda the size of an almond. Next day, boil for 20 minutes and when cold, take out all bones, keeping the bird in shape. Stuff with bread, sage and onion seasoning. Do not sew the bird up, but insert it inside the rabbit. Sew up rabbit and bake. Serve hot or cold.

TO TAN SKINS WITH WATTLE BARK: Soak skins in water till quite soft, then remove all fat and flesh. Half fill a kerosene tin with finely chopped wattle bark, fill the tin with hot water, and let stand for two days. Reduce liquid to the colour of weak tea and put in a tub, or other vessel, to well cover the skins. Turn skins every day and when liquid gets too weak add more tan, and continue this treatment for about three weeks, when the skin should be tanned. It is most important not to have the tan too strong, or it will harden the skins.

SISTER BEATRICE'S LEMONADE
3 lb. sugar, 1 oz. tartaric acid, 1 teaspoon of lemon, 2 pints water, juice and rind of 6 to 8 lemons, saltspoon Epsom salts.

Peel rind thinly. Squeeze lemons. Place all ingredients in a saucepan. Bring to boil and boil 3 minutes. Strain and bottle. Serve with iced water and fresh lemon slices.

and Cliff cycled from Riccarton to join the guests at the celebra-
tion. A photograph taken that day shows Marjorie on the cusp of
womanhood. Her curled hair is held back from her face with a
ribbon, tied girlishly in a bow. The dress she wears is one she made
herself from blue crepe, with a wide frilly collar and a U-shaped
inset of blue lace at the neckline. Pinned to the collar is a bouquet
of imitation flowers, and in her arms is the birthday cake made for
her by Aunt Amy. She looks both innocent and sturdy. Her jaw,
forearms, hands, hips all look strong, perfectly adapted for the hard
work she has ahead of her. I wonder how clearly she apprehended,
in that moment, that she was standing on the brink of her adult life.
For in just a few months' time she would be leaving her childhood,
her job, her town and her maiden name behind her.

Marjorie on her twenty-first birthday.

(from a foreword to *Marjorie Blackwell at Home*)
Visitors to Campbell Town passing that remarkably artistic home
of yours cannot fail to wonder what goes on inside, and your book
now supplies the answer. Enterprise such as yours is all too rare
these days; you have brought credit to our town.

    Reginald Taylor, Warden, Municipality of Campbell Town

CAMPBELL TOWN – by me

CAMPBELL Town, Campbell Town, the town of memories sweet,

AND green clad vales, and timbered hills, which every eye may greet,

MAY every one that lives here, enjoy the place like me;

PLAINS filled with sheep and tall gum trees so beautiful to see.

BEAUTIFUL rivers to sit by, with picnic grounds galore,

ELEGANT churches, historic buildings, could you wish for anything more?

LUXURIOUS cafes, recreation grounds and clubs for young and old.

LONELINESS is never heard of, or that's what I've been told.

THE Area School and all the shops and even the lovely Hall,

OR the popular swimming pool, and Gatty Memorial tall,

WILL take a lot of beating, I'm telling you my dear,

NO place is any nicer, Is it because my home is here?

2

Marjorie Blackwell

O N October 27, 1938, 21-year-old Marjorie Pearsall woke up in her small attic room at Riccarton without any particular sense of anticipation. It was a Thursday, a regular working day that she would have expected to spend cooking the Lyne household's meals. Perhaps, as Marjorie descended the stairs and entered the kitchen that morning, she thought of her fiancé, Cliff Blackwell, who'd gone shearing on the mainland. Two months had passed since he'd taken leave from employment at Riccarton, presumably in order to earn some extra cash that would go towards meeting the expenses of setting up house with Marjorie.

While Cliff had been away Marjorie had continued to spend all her free time decorating the Campbell Town house that was to be their home. But though she was implementing every fine detail of her plans for the home she would occupy as a wife, it seems she had not yet begun to plan in earnest for her day as a bride. If she had dreamed of being wed in white, then the gown had not made it beyond her imagination. If she had a particular date or church

Marjorie Blackwell in the late 1940s with her husband, Cliff, and sons, Gerald (at the rear) and Ross. Both boys were conceived on her birthday and born on January 20, four years apart.

or type of flowers in mind, all of these plans were eclipsed on that Thursday when the telephone rang in the hallway at Riccarton. It was Cliff, calling from somewhere in northern Tasmania, probably Launceston.

> All he said was, 'Get dressed and be on the midday train, as I'll be on it, and we are going to Hobart to get married.' I told him I'd have to ask Mrs Lyne first, and if she said I couldn't go I wouldn't be on the train.

Marjorie bargained for some time off and phoned her sister Doreen in Hobart, asking her for a place to stay for the night and to arrange a clergyman. She threw some clothes into a suitcase, either packing or wearing the navy blue suit that would be her wedding attire. Mrs Lyne agreed to drive her to the station—but just before they left Cliff phoned again, to tell Marjorie not to get on the train, as he'd managed to get a lift through to Hobart in a car and would pick her up at the station.

Perhaps, at the time, there was something romantic about the impetuous rush of their nuptials, but Marjorie would later reflect that she would have preferred a planned wedding, with guests and all the trimmings. Doreen, after taking her sister's phone call from Riccarton, must have swung into action. She prepared a celebratory evening meal and made up a bed with baby booties inside and a bell tied underneath. And although she was successful in arranging at short notice the services of the reverend of the Swan Street Methodist Church, the church itself turned out to be unavailable. Marjorie and Cliff, arriving in Hobart around nightfall, were half an hour later than expected, and the church's choir had begun its evening practice. So the reverend took the young couple back to his home and married them there. Marjorie became a blushing bride when Cliff embarrassed her by tickling her hand and making her laugh during the solemn ceremony.

———

Although Marjorie and Cliff had rushed to obtain the licence that would officially sanction their sharing of a bed, it would still be some months before they could sleep together comfortably. Despite their assumption that they'd be allowed to bunk up back at Riccarton, the newlyweds soon found that their employers expected them to retain their separate rooms—Marjorie in the house, sharing with the maid, and Cliff in a hut out in the grounds.

And what a crude, rough room that was. A small stretcher, no sheets, only blankets, no wardrobe or table but there was a chair and an open fireplace. One night, on the maid's day off, I crept across the yard into

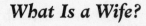

What Is a Wife?

When a little girl puts aside her dolls and games for dreams, dates and boys, she becomes a young woman and when she seriously concentrates all the dreams and all the dates on THE boy, it's only a matter of time before she turns into a wife. A girl becomes a wife with her eyes wide open. She knows that the sweetest words, "I take thee to be my wedded Husband," really mean, "I promise thee to cook three meals a day for years and years, thee will I worry about, brag about, and talk to, even when thou art not listening." A wife is a girl whose doll is wrapped in tissue and packed away in the closet, a girl with a packet of letters at the bottom of her glove box, and a snapshot album that is never opened – each a fragile link with girlhood, each so treasured and so forgotten. She has stepped from the leisurely, lovely period of girlhood into the hurried world of domesticity.

A wife is a Jill of all trades. She is a painter, judge, nurse, banker, secretary, and treasurer, a gardener, laundress, cook, and bureau of information. She can repair a toaster, put up a shelf, unstop a sink, remodel last year's coat, let down a hem, paper a wall, and make supper for a guest out of scraps from the refrigerator. When the going is really tough and something has to be done in a hurry, she can become a delicate flower, a siren, a lady wrestler, or a Mother Superior.

A wife likes new dresses and hats, going places, teas, shows, neighbours, furniture (provided it is moved sufficiently), soap, babies, parties, lettuce, novels, chatting, rainy nights, kittens, tub baths, other people's birthdays, a husband who comes home on time, and surprises that are gift wrapped. She is cool towards boxing matches, moths, mice, men drivers, cluttered workshops, grey hairs, telling her age, fried foods, unwashed children, camping trips, and the kind of women she knows her husband stares at.

the hut intending to sleep with Cliff until perhaps midnight, but no sooner had we both got into the stretcher, than the door opened and in walked Mr Lyne.

Marjorie tried to conceal herself under the blankets, probably unsuccessfully, while the owner of the property talked with Cliff. It was a humiliating experience, and the last of Marjorie's after-dark forays to the hut. On another occasion the couple attempted to spend an undisturbed night together in a single bed in a spare bedroom at Cliff's parents' home, but in the morning Cliff's father stormed in, took hold of Marjorie and dragged her out of bed because she and Cliff hadn't roused themselves by 8 a.m. So, when at last the Campbell Town home was ready, it was an excited and relieved Marjorie and Cliff who left Riccarton behind, ready to strike out on their own.

—⋙⋘—

Today, Campbell Town is a nest of coffee shops and petrol stations competing for the trade of Highway 1's north–south commuters. On either side of the impressively wide central strip is an architectural melange of the colonial and the contemporary, jumbled up with mid-twentieth-century municipal buildings and monuments whose pretensions to stateliness are undercut by their slightly downscale dimensions. It seems always to have been the quintessence of a small town.

The first five years of Marjorie and Cliff's marriage, spent in a small house fronting Campbell Town's busy main road, were its finest. For now, at least, the two young people were sexually compatible and drawn together by shared dreams: creating a home and beginning a family. Cliff's working life centred on practical and physical pursuits, such as woodcutting, truck driving and shearing. As well as being recreational, his fishing and shooting trips contributed to the provisioning of the household. Marjorie, 'brimming over with ideas, and bursting to put them into practice', relished the role of housewife and brought in her share of the income by catering for the needs of a fairly constant stream of lodgers. These were teachers, bank clerks, carpenters, and the wives and children of men receiving treatment at the nearby military hospital. Sometimes Marjorie had as many as four lodgers in the house, plus children, and she often did their washing and ironing. It's hard to imagine that there could have been much privacy or peace in the small house on the main road. Nevertheless, in 1940, eighteen months after their wedding, Marjorie and Cliff conceived a child. Marjorie confidently records that the conception took place on April 14 of that year—on her twenty-third birthday.

The birth she endured, the following January, was of the lonely, frightening kind all too common in her era. Largely alone in the local hospital, she was embarrassed by vomiting up the bowlful of green peas that she'd eaten during some pre-labour cravings, though her mortification paled into insignificance once the pain began in earnest. 'Not until I die,' she writes, 'will I ever forget those hours and hours of suffering, with no one to tell me what to do, or when.' After a twelve-hour labour Gerald Clifford Blackwell was born—a strapping baby boy weighing in at 9 lb, 13 oz (4.45 kg). In the wake of the traumatic birth, Marjorie vowed that this child would be her one and only.

Cough Mixture

Mix together 2 teaspoons each of olive oil, glycerine and honey with 4 teaspoons of orange juice. Shake before using. (For babies, ½ teaspoon four-hourly.) Or, equal quantities of rum and olive oil mixed together. A dessertspoon every two hours is correct dose.

As a young mother Marjorie adhered to the firm ideas of parenting that were prevalent at the time—keeping to strict routines and parking her baby outside for daytime naps. Gerald slept in a nook in the garden, unless it was raining, in which case he would be moved to the veranda. In those early baby days that many women experience in a fog of sleep deprivation and lactation hormones, Marjorie was as mindful as ever of the preciousness of her time. Though she breastfed Gerald, she did not 'waste' the long hours devoted to nursing. Instead, she chose a lounge chair for feeding so that she could rest her arms on the wide arms and knit while her baby suckled. (I have attempted, and failed, to replicate this feat of dexterity and determination.)

Whooping Cough

When whooping cough was raging in Campbell Town, when my two sons, Gerald and Ross, were children, they escaped it because I put slices of garlic on the soles of their feet (inside their socks), renewing it as the juice left it. In a few days, their breath smelt of garlic. It is a powerful cure of all manner of things.

Gerald grew to be a beautiful child: blond, bonny and affectionate. He won the hearts of his parents' friends and relatives, most especially Marjorie's childless Aunt Ruby, who frequently came from Launceston for weekends. Ruby, says Marjorie, wanted to hold the baby all the time, cried when he cried, and would sulk and refuse to eat if Marjorie gave him a smack. 'I was all the week getting Gerald back to form those days,' Marjorie recalls.

As it turned out, there would be a second child, another boy: Ross William Blackwell. According to Marjorie, Ross too was conceived on her birthday (her twenty-seventh). As well as being conceived on the same date as his brother, Ross timed his birth to perfection. He was born on January 20, 1945, Gerald's fourth birthday. The birth was little improvement on the first. Weighing in at 10 lb, 1 oz

ABC OF HAPPY MARRIAGE

ALWAYS. No refunds if not satisfied, so choose carefully.

BOREDOM. The arch enemy of marriage. Root it out at first signs of growth.

CHILDREN. Marriage was instituted for protection and procreation.

DOMESTIC DUTIES. The most important work in the whole community.

EXERCISE. Physical – to keep you trim. Mental – to keep you interesting.

FOOD. Be imaginative, original and appreciative.

GOSSIP. Don't gossip about your partner's failings.

HONESTY. Be honest with each other, but not brutal.

INTELLIGENCE. Allied with commonsense, it solves many problems.

JOB. A helping hand or listening ear when necessary.

KINDNESS. Be kind to each other.

LOVE. To marry for less is to invite disaster.

MODESTY. Something you can't afford to lose.

NAGGING. Never accomplishes anything. Try encouragement instead.

OTHERS. To live in a cocoon of self-centredness is not wise.

PRIDE. Something you can't afford to lose.

QUARRELS. Always apologise first, even if you are right.

RELIGION. The tie that binds, the anchor that holds.

SEX. Sexual compatibility is essential to a happy union.

TROUBLE. Meet it together with courage and loyalty.

UNDERSTANDING. When grounded in love it is never abused.

VINDICTIVE. Check it by a check-up on your physical relationship.

WEDDING DAY. A beautiful memory, but only the beginning.

XTRAVAGANCE. Stimulating occasionally, but must not become a habit.

YOU. Retain your personality. Refuse to become just Mum or Dad.

ZZZZZZZ. Unfortunately, there is no known cure for snoring.

(4.56 kg), Ross was a large baby who presented in the breech position; his birth necessitated many stitches and caused lasting pain that kept Marjorie on her back for many days.

But while the two boys' conceptions and births were uncannily synchronised, the four years separating them made all the difference in the circumstances. Though Marjorie would not have been the first or last woman to declare in the aftermath of labour that her first child would be her only one, I have a sense that she meant what she said. Ross has been a great source of joy to Marjorie throughout his life, but in her autobiography she records that he 'was conceived against [her] wishes'. She also pinpoints her second pregnancy as the end of happiness in her marriage to Cliff. 'My love', she says, 'was killed' at that time.

We can only imagine Cliff's perceptions of the marriage and its difficulties, but it's possible through Marjorie's account to locate the fault lines that destabilised the partnership. One was that Cliff and Marjorie were fundamentally mismatched in their expectations of their standard of living. Cliff appears to have been a rough-and-tumble country boy, and content to remain so, while Marjorie wanted more: more nice things, more refinement, more pleasure, romance and excitement. Marjorie wanted to go dancing; Cliff wanted to go bush. Her aspirations may not have been immensely lofty or materialistic, but she did place considerable emphasis on appearances and was prepared to work extremely hard in order to be able to afford the finer things in life. As Marjorie matured she developed increasingly strong ideas both about how one ought to live, and about how one ought to be seen to live, and Cliff was

Gerald's and Ross's shared birthday was a major annual event on the Blackwell calendar.
Here, Gerald turns five and Ross one.

always getting in the way of putting these ideas into practice. He would 'humiliate' her by turning up to events in filthy clothes and she would sometimes, when entertaining, lay out brown paper over one section of her best embroidered tablecloths so that his greasy arms didn't soil her napery.

Reading between the lines of Marjorie's descriptions of the many 'disappointments' she suffered at the hands of her husband, it seems likely that Cliff knew precisely where the pressure points were. In Marjorie's world the observance of birthdays, anniversaries, Christmas, Mother's Day and Father's Day has always been sacrosanct. Throughout her life she has kept precise track of who has remembered, who has not, and which gifts have been given ('The boys never missed giving me presents . . . and I still have the gifts—marcasite watch for Mother's Day 1951, a music box from Gerald, and lots of electrical goods, once he was earning; china animals, a flimsy feminine dressing gown from Ross in 1964 and a record "I love you more and more every day" in 1965'). Marjorie is very clear that she likes to receive her gifts on her birthday, and not a day before or after. Not only did Cliff rarely give gifts—he was also a reluctant recipient. Marjorie writes that Cliff often neglected to turn up to his own birthday parties, which she

Baby Entertained

I kept my babies entertained whilst busy by putting them in front of a mirror. They "talk" away to the other "baby".

Children Sick

Give them a whistle they can blow when they need attention, as a child's voice is weak and difficult to hear if they are sick.

staged annually on March 17, and also that it was his habit to leave his birthday and Christmas presents unopened. For a time she and the boys would open Cliff's gifts for him, but they eventually hit on the idea of leaving his presents unwrapped and re-presenting them at the next occasion. 'In the '50s, he had the same present for six years,' Marjorie reports.

It wasn't only Cliff who had birthday parties under duress: Marjorie took responsibility for the birthday festivities of a number of elderly widowed gentlemen from around the district. Far from relishing the annual visitation from Mrs Blackwell and her friends, one old hermit found the experience most aggravating—'he never appreciated it,' Marjorie recalls. For his last birthday, his ninety-eighth, Marjorie organised cups, saucers, cake, tablecloth, tea, sugar, milk, spoons and a handful of visitors to turn up at the old man's basic two-room shack.

> [He] was cantankerous all evening . . . [He] was going to pull the cloth off the table, throw the cake out the door, pour the tea on the floor, and so it went on. We all ate, but he never put one crumb in his mouth. However I managed to get a photo of him wielding a poker . . .

FOR THE CHILDREN'S PARTY TABLE

Candlesticks:

Open a tin of preserved pineapple. Put slices on a bread and butter plate. Peel bananas, cut about 2 inches off one end. Push a banana into the centre of the pineapple slice (through the hole). Place on to a plate. Place a crystallised cherry on top of banana to represent flame. Peel an orange with orange peeler. Take about 3 inches of peel. Push one end in with the banana, the other end under the slice of pineapple to represent handle.

Fill small moulds with red jelly. When set, turn out onto small plates. Peel small bananas, cut 2 inches off one end and split the other. Place a blanched almond coloured with cochineal inside the split to represent flame. Scoop a round hole in the middle of the jelly. Insert banana. If not firm, melt the scooped out piece and pour around to make it firm. Decorate base of jelly with whipped cream. Different coloured jelly candlesticks look most attractive on the table.

Trees in Tubs:

Buy some ice cream cones. Make some jellies and when at the setting stage, pour into cones. Stand cones upwards in a cake cooler to set. Pour made jelly into small moulds also to set, and for serving in. (Peanut butter jars are excellent). Get some fairly long tooth picks or clean sticks, push one end in the cones of jelly. Have some jelly almost set, dip cones in it, covering all. Dip into hundreds and thousands and put away to set once again. When set, push stick down into "tub" of jelly. Will look like miniature trees.

(from) GAMES AT THE PARTY
MATCHBOX RELAY

Two teams face each other in rows. The first person in each row places the cover part of an ordinary matchbox over his or her nose. At a given signal he must transfer it to the next player's nose without touching it with his hands. If the box falls to the ground he can replace it on his own nose and start again. The team which manages to get its matchbox on to the last player's nose is the winner.

Balloons

To blow up a large number of balloons, put the vacuum cleaner hose on the blowing end of the machine.

Marjorie took this snap of a 98-year-old Campbell Town recluse on his last birthday.
Though the old man 'never appreciated it', Marjorie celebrated his birthday each year.

Public outings of all kinds seem to have provided Cliff with an arena in which to retaliate for whatever wrongs he felt he had suffered behind closed doors. When Marjorie bought train tickets for the family to go to Launceston to see the Queen, Cliff failed to turn up at the station until the train was pulling out. When Marjorie organised for the family to go to Launceston to see the American evangelist Billy Graham, it was only Marjorie and the boys who eventually went through the gates. Marjorie would walk into church to attend a wedding, find a seat and then look around to find that Cliff was no longer with her. Marjorie (who couldn't at this time drive a car) would be waiting with the boys to make a trip to visit

Apple Trick for Children

To settle the old argument over the bigger piece of apple, allow one child to cut it in halves and the other to have first pick.

relatives, and Cliff wouldn't show up to take them. The same scenario played out time and time again: Marjorie would have everything organised, and Cliff would be nowhere to be seen.

Cliff was a generous man, hardworking and tough, and Marjorie liked these aspects of his character (except when his generosity landed her with debts). She writes admiringly of how, while in the middle of ploughing a paddock, he had a tooth pulled without any numbing agent and returned immediately to his work. She liked his resourcefulness—the way he made his bootlaces out of kangaroo hide, and how he could fix just about anything. But although she admired his toughness, as the years went by Marjorie was increasingly frustrated by his physical and social 'roughness'. She found his style of football playing 'rough'; she found him to be 'rough' with his work equipment, machinery and clothes. There were skirmishes between the Blackwells over moral standards in parenting, too. Cliff thought it was perfectly okay for his young sons to watch dogs mating, but Marjorie found this unacceptable. ('You are only jealous because you are not the bitch,' Cliff is supposed to have sniped back at her on one occasion.) Cliff, however, seems to have had a prim streak of his own concerning his wife's clothing: a knee-length divided tennis skirt was on the wrong side of his standards of propriety.

Finger Paint for Children

Make a paste with cornflour and cold water. Add boiling water and stir until it thickens. Divide, and put different food colourings into several portions.

The marriage had more serious problems than these. According to Marjorie's accounts, Cliff grew up in a family afflicted by domestic violence, and it seems that he brought this legacy into his own marriage.

While the violence appears to have intensified as the years went on, Marjorie reports that there were times even in the early days of her marriage to Cliff when she felt unsafe. There were 'jokes', she recalls, that didn't strike her as particularly funny:

> One I recall was the day when I was helping him get a load of wood up in the bush, and he turned to me and said, 'You know Petty (that's what he called me). If I was to kill you and bury you up here with the bulldozer, no one would know who did it, or ever find you. I could say you cleared out and left me.'

Another time, when they were driving slowly through floodwaters, Cliff stopped the car so Marjorie could open the door and see how deep the water was. 'You know, I could push you out and drown you, and people would think it was an accident,' Cliff reportedly said.

For Marjorie, who 'craved love and affection', the shortcomings of her marriage only deepened her hunger for appreciation and affirmation. Initially, it was motherhood and home-making that provided the focus for her copious energy and desire for approval. Rather than managing household chores around the needs of children (as seems these days to be the expectation that stay-at-home parents with young children have of themselves), Marjorie managed her boys around her need to complete—largely single-handedly—many onerous daily chores. In addition to all the provisioning,

Painting (children's)
Hang behind their doors on the clip-type skirt hangers.

Photograph of Baby
When he's able to sit up for a photograph, stick some cellulose tape on the palm of his hands. The antics while trying to remove it are delightful.

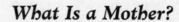

What Is a Mother?

A mother is a wonderful creature constructed almost entirely of love and this she can express in a million ways, from hugs and kisses, and good cooking, and patient listening, to stern lectures, strict rules, and repeated uses of the word "No!".

Like snowflakes, no two mothers are alike, but they have a number of things in common. Name anything . . . a mother can be found washing it, roasting it, polishing it, getting rid of it, repairing it, spanking it, packing it, teaching it, redecorating it, loving it, or talking it over at P and F [Parents and Friends, the Australian equivalent of the PTA].

A mother cares about, and for, almost everything; gardens, pets, the state of the nation, the worn spot on the rug, hungry people, and most of all "Father" and her children. For these she can do anything, dare anything, and fight for anything necessary to their happiness. A mother is not always an angel. She will often disagree with you . . . expect too much of you . . . question your choice of friends . . . and bring up the subject of work when you feel the least energetic. But she is always ready to help when you need her.

God made mothers more special than anyone else. He made them the bearers of life and in so doing, knew they had to be more exceptional than the rest of us. He made them the cornerstone of the home, the foundation of the family, the backbone of society, the ideal of all that is best with the human race. God couldn't be everywhere so he made mothers. They are the guardians of decency, the preservers of peace, the upholders of truth, the protectors of morality, the symbol of virtue, an inspiration to all that is noble and good in life, and love knows no greater representative than that of a mother's love. Upon our earth, no title is more revered and no sound more beautiful or sweeter heard than the tender loving word – mother.

Mothers are the daughters of yesterday, the grandmothers of tomorrow and the hope of today. Mothers are the closest to God one can feel while passing through this world's great story.

Marjorie made most of Gerald's and Ross's clothes by hand,
including these knitted fair isle sweaters.

cooking and house cleaning, and the washing, ironing and making
of clothes, Marjorie had to deal with livestock. Each afternoon
she would bring in her cows for the night, and generally she would
take Gerald and Ross with her on the muster. When it was raining
she would leave the boys at home, tethered by their 'leads' to the
legs of the kitchen table. Discipline in the Blackwell home was
unashamedly authoritarian, too, and the boys' punishments ranged
from 'the strap' to being shut in a cupboard under the stairs until
they were sorry. Marjorie recalls that her sons were of quite distinct
temperaments—Ross would tough out his punishments with barely
a murmur, whereas the more sensitive Gerald would cry.

Like many mothers, then and now, Marjorie felt that her children's
appearance and manners were a measure of her own competence. She
sewed or knitted most of her boys' clothing, hand-making everything

The Ideal Mother

They said: "Describe the ideal Mother", so I thought I'd have a try
We all would like to be her, but the goal is pretty high.
She's always kind and loving. She's patient – strong but fair,
She has a sense of humour – and she doesn't mind long hair!
Her house is all in order, and her cupboards neat and tidy –
I can't imagine her forgetting to buy her meat on Friday!
She knows where all the socks are (even has them in their pairs)
And doesn't need to plan the meal as she listens to the prayers.

Describe the ideal Mother? I can see her now so easily
She's cheerful, gay and happy, even when the kids are measly.
"Please listen to my reading"; "How do you do these sums?"
"Mother, what does 'bliss' mean?" "Mum, how do you spell 'succumbs'?"
Yes, this mother gets it also, but it doesn't make her dizzy,
She wouldn't say "Ask Father", or "Run away, I'm busy."
She can do the latest dances; she knows all the Top Ten hits;
Her garden is a picture, she can make a dress that fits.

Her children are contented – they wouldn't dream of fighting,
She asks the hardest riddles, and her stories are exciting.
Her tins are never empty, and her mending's up to date;
She's pretty good at cricket, and she's even learned to skate.
Her clothes are not too "with it" (she knows how to be her age).
Her husband thinks she's great, because she keeps within his wage.
Oh Boy, the Ideal Mother – She's enough to turn all heads!
But that's enough day-dreaming – I haven't made the beds!

FOR PARTY TABLE

Rub spots of lacquer of different colour on nine or ten mothballs, and put them in a tall glass bowl with half a gallon of cold water, one and a half teaspoons baking powder or carb. soda, and ¾ teaspoon of tartaric acid. Put bowl in centre of table and the solution will cause the balls to rise and fall for about three hours.

from their handkerchiefs to their dressing gowns, even stitching slippers out of rabbit skin.

> Without fear of contradiction I can say that my boys were two of the best-dressed children in the town. I revelled in making them pretty clothes, like fair isle sweaters, cap and socks to match; trousers in tweed or velvet . . . I was forever being complimented on how I dressed and brought them up.

The boys' shared birthday made for an important annual production: a shared birthday party. The cake, a closely guarded secret until the very last minute, was always a feature. Over the years there were cakes concocted to feature a house, fence and animals; a garage and motor cars; Humpty Dumpty; the old woman who lived in a shoe; a football; a train and carriages; a merry-go-round. On Gerald's fourth birthday, the day Marjorie gave birth to Ross, the much-anticipated party wasn't cancelled or postponed. Rather, Marjorie blew up all the balloons and arranged all the trimmings before she went to hospital, and had Cliff's sister come in to set the table and supervise the party.

By 1948—the year Gerald turned seven and Ross three—Marjorie was ready to test out the standard of her home-making skills beyond the confines of her own four walls. Remembering her Riccarton days and her prize-winning pound of butter, Marjorie set her sights squarely on the trestle tables of the Campbell Town Show.

The rewards were immediate. That year, she entered a range of

Child in Hospital: Eliminate tearful goodbyes
when visiting a child in hospital; give a small surprise
gift at the end of the visit, then leave quickly.

items and came home with thirteen awards. By 1951 she had upped her score to twenty-six prizes and had bagged the W. T. Findlay silver cup for the most points gained by an exhibitor at the show: 'that really spurred me on. I was so excited I started right away to make things for the show the following year. I was well stocked by the next June, and this paid off as I came home with 36 prizes and again, the cup.'

Marjorie was competing across the range of domestic categories: cakes, preserves, sauces, chutneys, dripping, pickles, jams, cordials, confectionery, eggs, soap, sewing, knitting, embroidery, patchwork, photography, pot plants, rock gardens, vegetables. She was sufficiently satisfied with her achievements to take the year off in 1954, but due to overwhelming public demand ('people told me they missed my entries, and the benches were bare') she returned to the show in 1955, winning forty-four prizes and the cup. And there was still scope for improvement. In 1956 she won fifty-five prizes and the cup, in 1957 she won sixty-two prizes and the cup, and in 1958 she blitzed the field with her Campbell Town Show personal best: a phenomenal seventy-eight prizes and the cup.

While this outstanding success might suggest that the Campbell Town Show was Marjorie's preoccupation during the 1950s, in fact a greater part of her energy and creativity was devoted to the creation of a dream home. Built on the vacant corner block next door to Marjorie and Cliff's first home, the new place was to be the fulfilment of Marjorie's every aspiration for comfort and style, practicality and efficiency—the perfect backdrop for the model modern housewife. At the time the house was built the Blackwell marriage was hardly a picture of unity. However, in naming the home, Marjorie's romantic sensibilities triumphed over the material facts of her daily life. She concocted the name Climar from the first three letters of her given

HINTS IN RHYME

TO GET THAT SCREW

When a screw is in too tight,
And you've tried with all your might,
Though 'twon't loosen, don't resign,
Try this happy thought of mine:
Your screw-driver, get it hot –
This you'll find will help a lot.

STOP THAT LEAK

Leaking pipe is something you
Can't put off attending to.
With this trouble you can cope –
Use a piece of softened soap.
Soap will plug the leak, I've found,
Till the plumber comes around.

METHYLATED SPIRITS

Mixed with whitening 'tis a wheeze
To clean and shine your piano keys.
With methylated and soft duster,
Clean all the glass that you can muster,
And don't forget that mirrors, too,
When polished thus will shine like new.

name and Cliff's, and had this portmanteau moniker affixed to the front of the house in raised concrete.

Climar began life in Marjorie's imagination and on the scores of sheets of paper that she used in sketching out her ideas. Inspired by a house with curving walls that she had seen and loved in Launceston, Marjorie's sketches were turned into building plans by a draftsman. The inner walls were made from second-hand bricks, each one hand-cleaned by Marjorie herself, and the outer walls were of new bricks speckled in shades from apricot through to burnt orange. The floor plan was meticulously thought out and featured built-ins galore, including the cacti gardens that bordered the electric fire in the lounge and a semi-circular inset couch beneath a semi-circular showcase ('for nic-nacs and my silver cups'). For entertaining, glass concertina doors could be folded back to make one large space out of the dining room and lounge. Matching sandblasted designs adorned the glass dining-room doors and the curving glass expanse of the outer wall of the entrance hall. In the bathroom, the yellow rubber flooring was inset with a black rubber yacht modelled after the one Prince Charles had when he was a boy. 'The kitchen was "alive" with built-ins,' Marjorie writes: these included built-in flour and sugar bins. Other enviable features of the home included a laundry chute and a dedicated sewing room that led off from the kitchen.

Climar was four years in the making, and for this Marjorie blames the builders: 'they wasted time, talking, skylarking and smoking, and we paid for it.' For each of those years, Marjorie poured her soul into the finest details of her dream home. By the time she and her family moved in, there was not a single aspect of the design, decor, furnishings or contents that had been left to chance:

> My nerves were very frayed, watching the house slowly grow, from my sunroom window, and more especially, when the workmen didn't turn up for days on end. I sat every night embroidering tablecloths, pillowslips, even 36 linen tea-towels, made mats, stools, pictures, cushions, bed-spreads and new lingerie, so the contents matched the home, and as it neared completion and I was taking the things down bit by bit and installing them in their new home, my cup was overflowing; then the very night (a Tuesday) I was going to move in, I went down and lit the kitchen fire, turned every light on, sat in a chair and stared all around and was almost hysterical with joy. And I never had anyone to share that joy with me, as it was Empire Day (1955) and Cliff and the boys were too busy in the top paddock with their bonfire and crackers.

The exterior of the house was no less meticulously planned and executed. The approach to the front door was by way of a bridge

Fish:

3 or 4 grains of Conde's Crystals in the tank each week will keep tank clean. This is most important if you want healthy fish. A pinch of Epsom salts once a week stops the fish from becoming constipated. One meal a day in summer and one every week in winter is what a fish requires. As much as will lie flat on a threepence is sufficient for a 3-inch fish.

If the water turns green in aquarium the light is usually too bright. Try pasting some tissue paper on the side facing the light or introducing more plants.

Indigestion is the most common ailment with fish and is caused through constipation brought about through feeding the fish with too much starchy dried food. Give finely cut up earth worms occasionally or scraped raw meat. They also like boiled cabbage or spinach and finely cut lettuce.

Laces (lost)

Prevent lost laces by stitching them together where they first cross after being threaded into the shoe.

Pram Hint

If you want to bring baby's pram into the house but fear dirty wheel marks on carpet, try this: – Buy four shower caps and pull them over the pram wheels. There will be no marks and the plastic caps last for ages.

IF you want your pet to talk, a budgerigar must be no older than 4 weeks when purchased. Do not go near its cage for a week; it must have sufficient food and water for that period. By then it will have come accustomed to its surroundings and all fear and fright will be gone. Commence by saying one sentence such as "Hullo Joey", or "Good morning, boy", or whatever his name may be. Always say the same sentence until he has said it, then you can go ahead and teach it other sentences. In the evening is the best time, with the lights lowered. Place a cloth over the cage and insert your hand and tickle the bird's head, all the time repeating the one sentence. Keep your hand perfectly still if he takes fright and flies about his cage. Wait until he settles down and do it again. It will soon learn to enjoy it after a few nights.

You have heard some budgerigars saying a jumbled sentence, well, that is because they have said too many sentences to the bird at the beginning, instead of saying one until it has learned it perfectly.

Two birds in the one cage will never talk; there must be only one, preferably a male bird.

over a lily pond, and then by one or other of two flights of steps, divided by a flower garden. The house that Marjorie built quickly became an icon in Campbell Town, not least because of its unique wrought-iron and brick fence. Set out in the musical notation for 'Melody of Love', wrought-iron crotchets and minims are affixed to wrought-iron stave lines, each bar separated by a brick pillar. The wrought-iron gates are fashioned in the shape of piano accordions. Climar soon became a tourist attraction; buses and cars would pull up outside to allow the occupants to have a quick peek or take a photograph. Many people came to the front door and asked to have a look through the house, and Marjorie kept a visitors' book to record their glowing impressions. One poetess contributed the following lines:

> It's a friendly house by the friendly road, its doors are open wide,
> The joys pass in and the cares pass out—no room for cares inside.
> For kindness and love are the dwellers there, you are welcomed in
>   with pride,
> To the friendly house by the friendly road where peace and joy abide.

This was precisely what Marjorie wanted her visitors to see, but she was only too aware of the disjunction between the picture-perfect impression that she worked so strenuously to maintain and the reality of the emotional climate at Climar. 'Only God, and close relatives, friends, doctors and policemen know what went on behind the walls of our homes,' she writes ominously. Perhaps the white canary that lived in a cage on a stand in the hallway of Climar was more on the money than the visitors' book scribes: the tune he whistled was 'There's Nae Luck about the House'.

The late 1950s saw Marjorie ensconced in Climar, and compensating for the unhappiness of her marriage with a hectic round of entertaining, dancing and competing in the annual show. As the decade reached its close, the boys were nearing independence and Marjorie was ready to take on the working world. She picked up a job for which her local roots, doggedness and natural curiosity eminently qualified her: she became the Campbell Town stringer for the ABC. Before long she would be providing local content for Launceston's *Examiner* and Hobart's *Mercury* newspapers as well. 'I was always on the alert and news hungry and there was never a week day go past or a Sunday that I didn't pull up a bus with a package of news for the *Examiner*.'

While news editors seem to have been grateful for Marjorie's tenacity, some Campbell Town residents were on occasion less appreciative of the efforts of their neighbourhood paparazza. After photographing a blazing building Marjorie was chased down the street by the residents of the home, who tried to wrest the camera from her. Marjorie's coverage of the local school's fiery parents' and friends' meetings also created tensions. During meetings the headmaster would 'look daggers' at Marjorie, and if he attempted to keep anything off the record Marjorie immediately knew that it was 'A1 stuff' and took notes all the more diligently.

Choking

Try and hook out the obstruction with finger, or give a dry crust of bread. If these fail, give a dessertspoon of mustard in a cup of water to make the patient vomit. If a child, turn up-side-down and shake.

Slippers (toddler's)

Sew a small bell to your toddler's slippers and you'll know which way he is heading and he'll enjoy the noise as well.

Shampooing the Children's Hair

Put an inexpensive pair of swimming goggles on them and they will look forward to their hair being washed.

GERALD Clifford is my eldest son, just sixteen and a half years old,
Tall and healthy, full of vigour, and neither rude nor bold.
He hasn't taken to smoking, he won't wet his lips with drink,
He's fussy with food and watches his diet, lots of tea he'll never sink.
He's clean with his clothes and body, fusses over his teeth and hair.
Bathes regular without any asking – try closing his window, just dare.
Anniversaries are never forgotten with appropriate cards as well,
He never wastes his money, on arguments he'll never dwell.
Very seldom seen in a temper is this young lad of mine,
He laughs a lot more than he grumbles, his disposition is fine.
He never swears, listens to dirty yarns, his manners are pretty good.
And he loves all children and animals but that's easily understood.
Gerald is like me in ways and looks though he wasn't as good at school,
But never mind that, he's good to his Mum and follows the Golden Rule.
The nicest compliment that he's ever paid was the day he told me this –
'I hope my girl turns out like you and my life will be full of bliss.'
One of his names comes from father, the other a favourite of mine,
He was baptized at Ross on my birthday on a day so lovely and fine.
Gerald is excellent with machinery – could drive a truck when five,
And he doesn't like sport of any kind, but he can swim and dive.
He goes regularly to the pictures but hasn't yet learned to dance.
He has found himself a lady love – she sends him into a trance.
Gerald finds old folk as interesting as all his teenage friends,
He'll go out of his way to help others, it's on them his future depends.
Both sons are born on the same day and month, the 20th of January it falls,
It comes in handy at party time as for only one cake it calls.

Minties

Heat a tablespoon of butter, 2 rounded tablespoons of sugar, 3 tablespoons golden syrup, until dissolved. Remove from heat, add ½ teaspoon peppermint essence and 1½ cups full cream powdered milk. Beat well. Roll pieces between hands into sausage-like rolls. Twist like barley sugar, cut into lengths. Allow to set.

Insect in Ear

If someone around smokes, a puff into the ear will make the insect crawl out.

Leeches

When bushwalking take a jar of Vegemite with you. It puts the leech out of his misery faster than salt will ever do.

I'M composing this about my younger son who is twelve and a half years old,
His name is Ross William Blackwell, his hair is the colour of gold.
He takes after his dad in ways and looks, has an answer for everything.
He's full of wit, but not at school, where he likes to have a good fling.
Ross was a contented baby, the neighbours seldom heard him cry.
From morn to night he slept or cooed, my – how the time doth fly.
He wouldn't be cuddled at babyhood, he preferred to be alone,
And he'll never tell of his successes or you never hear him moan.
Ross sings himself to sleep at night and wakes up doing the same.
And whistles and sings all day as well – for that I am to blame.
He's been extremely healthy and rarely gets a cold,
And loves his game of football – being tough, he's hard to hold.
He rises bright and early, goes to bed without being told,
Cleans his teeth and brushes his hair – in his drawer his clothes he does fold.
His manners are not so brilliant, his memory is nearly as bad,
But he's not a sis or a sooky, so that makes me very glad.
Ross likes all kind of craft work, whether it's at home or school,
He won a swimming certificate, right down at our local pool.
His reading matter is comics, every serial he knows on the air,
He climbs, he jumps, he even slides, and all he puts on he'll tear.
The pictures he follows up closely and likes the ones that are funny,
For milking the cow and getting the sticks, he gets five bob pocket money.
He's brave with a doctor or dentist – goes alone, without parent aid,
But he has a lovely temper, that comes from the stock he was made.
Why did we call him Ross William – well that's easy to explain,
My home town is the hamlet of Ross – William, both his grandfathers' name.

Dinners Kept Hot

Place foil over dinner and put in moderate oven or over a pot of water.

Matches: If you can't keep a box of matches in the kitchen, cut away about a third of the top of the box. The matches are still satisfactory for household use, but men won't carry a box likely to spill.

Carbon Paper: If carbon paper is worn, hold near fire until warm. The heat will spread the carbon evenly on worn patches and so give it a new lease of life.

UMBRELLAS REVIVED:
Umbrellas can be revived if you sponge them with a tablespoon sugar diluted in ½ pint boiling water.

The year Marjorie turned forty-two, 1959, brought with it difficulties and conflicts that would have lasting consequences. It was during that year that Marjorie's son Gerald found himself, aged eighteen, at the altar marrying his 'school-girl sweetheart'. For a time he and his new wife lived at Climar, but before long they settled next door, in the house that had been Marjorie and Cliff's first home. Marjorie, usually so attentive to detail, doesn't note in her autobiography the date of Gerald's wedding. She does, however, record that the couple's first son was born on March 15, 1960. The timing of marriages and births has long been the domain of small-town gossips, and Marjorie records the doings of certain Campbell Town 'busybodies' who marked wedding and birth dates on their calendars, and surveyed the landscape through binoculars to spy nappies on washing lines and observe young ladies' visits to the doctor. She seems to suggest that Gerald and his wife became the targets of this kind of gossip, and if this was the case it must have been difficult for them—and for Marjorie, the model mother and housewife—to bear.

It was also in 1959 that Cliff, who had suffered numerous injuries in his life of hard manual labour, suffered a serious accident. While helping to transport an old Hobart tram to a property near the central Tasmanian hamlet of Interlaken, Cliff was struck on the head by a falling crane. His jaw broken and his mouth torn open, he was taken to hospital in Hobart, where he had his jaw wired and his wound stitched. When he was released from hospital he had to be fed liquefied food through a plastic tube. Marjorie nursed him in the aftermath of his accident, but the injury marked the point when her relations with Cliff took their final, irrevocable turn for the worse.

Though we have no record of Cliff's version of events, Marjorie has recorded in detail her view of their increasingly serious conflicts. She writes of how he held her down and smelled her when she returned home from dances, to see whether or not she had been with another man; how she buried guns in the garden after being threatened; and how she 'dreaded bed time' and sometimes stayed up all night because she had become 'rattled with blaspheming'.

If things weren't bad enough on the home front, there was also the public drama of the 1959 Campbell Town Show. It's hard to tell from Marjorie's autobiography precisely what occurred during the prize-giving ceremony, but the events left Marjorie feeling deeply wronged. It appears that although Marjorie won seventy-two prizes (only six shy of her record, attained the previous year) and should have been awarded the W. T. Findlay silver cup for the most points earned by an exhibitor, the cup was not forthcoming. Marjorie must have looked for it in the lead-up to the ceremony, only to find that it was missing from the silverware. Only the perpetual cup (one that was kept for twelve months) was visible, but it was high up on a shelf behind wire netting.

Motivated by an ardent ambition to have the cup for domestic

Chickens Hatched in Electric Frypan

Place an asbestos mat in the frypan which has been previously heated to 99.9°, at which temperature the frypan should remain until hatching is completed. Place dish filled with cotton wool on mat and arrange eggs (about 5) comfortably, packed, but not touching each other in the dish of cotton wool, standing them on their pointed ends and slightly slanting. Place another dish of water in the frypan and put on the lid. Every 12 hours turn the eggs and allow them to slant the opposite way. Hatching takes approximately 3 weeks. As chickens emerge from the shells, raise the lid of the frypan very slightly to allow ventilation. The whole operation should be carried out in a warm room free of draughts. A second frypan heated to just warm and inverted but propped up to allow air to pass through, may be used to cover the chicks when hatched. A box with holes punched in its lid and kept in a warm place may be used if a second frypan is not available.

entries presented to her by the governor of Tasmania, as did the winners of the livestock categories, Marjorie had a tall reporter get it down from the shelf behind the netting. By some means she managed to get the perpetual cup presented to her by the governor, but in her oblique account of these happenings she alleges that she suffered 'physically' in order to achieve her ambition, and that she needed the help of 'staunch sympathisers' in order to recover from the 'trauma'. Marjorie did not enter the show in 1960, 1961 or 1962.

Unfortunately, Marjorie's daily diaries from this period have not survived to shed more light on proceedings— but whatever occurred in 1959, it led to the withdrawal of the W. T. Findlay cup for most points in the show. The

The house that Marjorie built: Climar, Campbell Town, in its heyday. Joker, at left, was Marjorie's 'second-favourite dog'.

organisers offered to give Marjorie the perpetual cup for keeps, and to have it engraved with the years she had won most points in the show, presumably to placate her. Marjorie accepted, though unwillingly.

It would take some time for her to recognise the silver lining of the dark clouds of the 1959 show debacle: the end of her involvement with the Campbell Town Show would prove to be the beginning of her life as an author.

> It was over that to-do and jealousy that I decided to write my first book, as I thought that if I could not be happy doing entries for the Show, I might be able to make someone else happy by sharing my secrets of success. So I sat day in and day out at the book, happy to know that now they did not have to have their secret meetings with me being the topic of conversation.

And so *Marjorie Blackwell at Home* was born. Written during the 1960s hiatus in Marjorie's competitive show career, and released in 1965, the cookbook and multi-purpose advice manual was turned down by two publishers on the grounds that there were too many cookbooks already on the market, but Marjorie soon secured an agreement with the Launceston printery Foot & Playsted. It seems that Marjorie herself took responsibility for the distribution of the book and that initially she found booksellers reluctant to stock it. Cookbooks, they said, were slow to sell. But *Marjorie Blackwell at Home* defied the trend and flew off Tasmanian bookshop shelves until it sold out. The public notice she generated during this period led to Marjorie's appearance in the pages of the *Australian Women's Weekly*, a publication she much admired. Only a thousand copies of *Marjorie Blackwell at Home* were printed and Marjorie owns just a single copy; second-hand copies are highly sought-after.

Held together with the spiral binding that makes it so practical

(from) *Knitting Hints*

When knitting children's sweaters or cardigans, commence from top of sleeve instead of cuffs. In this way the cuff can be unpicked and sleeve lengthened quite easily. Follow the knitting pattern by reversing the directions, increasing where it states decreasing, and vice versa.

Use a second ball of wool and double-knit over elbow section when knitting children's pullovers. Then you will be sure to get the last bit of wear from your efforts.

Knit some shirring elastic in with the wool when knitting the tops of boys' sox to keep them fitting snugly.

Crochet and knitting needles should be washed occasionally with soap and water. This lets you work faster and easier.

Keep your hands smooth and soft when knitting or doing crochet work by rubbing a little talc powder into them every now and then. Absorbs the sweat. Keeps garments clean, too.

If you have to store wool, push a mothball into the centre.

When knitting with black wool, use white needles, and vice versa.

Snap a press stud at the beginning of a row of knitting you want to mark, instead of the usual pin.

For a firmer seam, start each row by knitting into backs of first stitch.

Spare balls of wool of the same ply can be used up by crocheting them into chains, then knitting on No. 3 needles into rugs or bulky sweaters. Gives a boucle effect.

If you come close to the end of a ball of wool during knitting and wonder if you have enough for another row of knitting, measure the length across the garment. If it is four times that width, you will have enough yarn for one more row.

Party Glasses

Party glasses for children can be made attractive by first dipping the rims into cold water or lemon juice, then into hundreds and thousands, or castor sugar. Write their names on them, too, with nail polish.

to use in the kitchen, the book's 310 pages are divided into forty-four sections covering everything from the basic categories of foods—Biscuits; Cakes; Fish Dishes; Jams, Jellies, Honey and Marmalades; Loaves and Teacakes; Meat Dishes; Pastry Recipes; Puddings (Summer); Puddings (Winter); Relish; Sauces and Ketchup; Scones, Coffee Rolls, Hot Cross Buns, Doughnuts and Pikelets; Sweets; Vegetables—to hints on pot plants, gardening, hosting 'beer parties', children's party cakes and games, health, prolonging the life of cut flowers, caring for pets, identifying cuts of meat, sewing, washing and treating stains. 'All these things,' writes Marjorie in the foreword, 'are dear to the heart and the majority of all women.'

Other than the occasional flourish of curling font, *Marjorie Blackwell at Home* is plainly designed. The recipes are not illustrated and, apart from a few line drawings and diagrams in the handcraft sections, the only images in the book are photographs of our heroine, her offspring and her home. Twelve of the sixteen photographs are of a smiling Marjorie, modestly dressed and sometimes aproned, posing with the fruits of her best-practice housewifery. Eleven fine upstanding citizens provided testimonials that grace the early pages of the volume. A federal politician of the day implores that the book be read in the context that 'the libraries of the world are its arsenals for the pursuit of knowledge and the defeat of ignorance', and the host of the ABC's *Tasmanian Country Hour Women's Session* dubs Marjorie 'Tasmania's

Cake Cutting

If cutting a sponge in two, place a coarse piece of cotton around the cake; fold both ends in one hand and pull through the cake. The result is a clean cut.

(from) *Hints for Show Cooks*

(Given me by Show Judges)

Cakes – Large, Plain: To ensure that the mixture, when cooked, will be nice and smooth, do not let the mixture curdle, when adding the eggs one by one to butter and sugar. To prevent this, just beat the eggs a little after each addition, and then quickly add about ¼ of the flour, and if there are risings in the ingredients, sift that with the flour, too, then beat well. You will know when the cake is cooked because it will leave the sides of the tin. (So will sponges and sandwiches.) Mix quickly and lightly.

Lamingtons: Use a butter cake foundation. Always leave a day or so before cutting into a 1½ inch square, or the same depth as the cake, so it will be a perfect square. Icing should be well flavoured and coloured nicely. It should be thick enough so as cake won't go soggy. My recipe for Lamington icing that I use at Show time (and I'm seldom beaten with Lamingtons) is made from the following ingredients: ½ lb. icing sugar, 1 level dessertspoon cocoa, 1 dessertspoon butter, 2 tablespoons boiling water. Dissolve butter in boiling water. Stir in icing sugar and place on stove until just warm, stirring all the time. Use quickly whilst warm. An easy way to cover with coconut is to place each as you ice them in a paper bag of coconut and shake well.

Scones: Cut with medium size cutter. Glaze with milk to ensure an even brown top and to remove surplus flour. Grease your tray, do not flour it. Knead lightly so as to have an even outer surface and a fine texture. Scones will run to one side if mixture is too moist or you lean on the cutter. Cook in hot oven 10 minutes. Always choose even size scones for a collection on the plate. Fruit scones should be cooked in a moderately hot oven as the fruit will burn. A perfect show scone should be well risen, evenly brown on top, of an even white, smooth texture and should have even sides without cracks. It should also be elastic to the touch.

Apron (novel) Nine men's ties sewn together make a nice waist apron. Cut ties in half and use the broad end, after unpicking back seam. Two of the smaller ends will act as ties and band.

> *"Don't expect success, if you make your cakes by guess."*

If you want a lighter sponge, replace a tablespoon of the flour with custard powder. Put them into tins with 8cm (3 inch) sides and they'll rise higher. Be sure when making them for a show that you have equal amounts of mixture in them. Weigh each tin of mixture. If you beat the bicarbonate of soda with the egg until it is frothy before you add the sugar, the sponge will be lighter.

If you have surplus liquid when cooking apples, use it instead of milk and you'll find you'll have a lovely light textured sponge, and use tepid water instead of cold, if recipe says water.

Always mix with metal spoon for best results.

To avoid failure when making a sponge cake, have the eggs at room temperature. Never use them straight from the refrigerator. Removing the sponge from the oven too soon will cause it to shrink after it has been out a while.

Toss fruit in cornflour (shake off surplus) before adding to a fruit cake, then it won't sink to the bottom as it's cooking.

When a recipe says 1 cup of flour, always spoon the flour into the cup – never dip the cup into the flour.

When icing a chocolate cake, grate dark chocolate straight on to top of cake as soon as it comes from the oven. Spread evenly with the flat of a knife then quickly sprinkle over chopped nuts or coconut.

When making a chocolate cake, mix the cocoa with a little warm water and add it instead of in its powder form. The cake isn't so dry then. Try also adding a dessertspoon of raspberry jam for a moister cake.

For easier creaming, heat the sugar and not the butter. Better results too.

To save eggs, dissolve 1 tablespoon gelatine in a little cold water, then enough boiling water to make a small cupful. Whisk to a froth. This is equal to 2 eggs. Also, in a plain cake, only one egg is needed, instead of 3, if you add 1 dessertspoon of vinegar; or substitute an egg with 2 tablespoons of vinegar mixed with 1 teaspoon bicarbonate of soda.

If a recipe says "rub butter into flour", grate the butter in. Better still if you've had the butter in the refrigerator.

Put a whole apple in the cake tin with your cake to keep it fresh and moist.

When making a butter cake put a dish of cold water on the lowest rung in the oven. It prevents the cake sticking to the tin, also from drying out on the bottom and burning.

If you have to cut cakes, as for Lamingtons, put them in freezer for an hour or so to firm, then the crumbs won't go into icing when you go to ice them.

Mrs Beeton' (a reference to the nineteenth-century British bestseller *Mrs Beeton's Book of Household Management*)—perhaps the earliest printed instance of this sobriquet. The Warden of the Municipality of Campbell Town congratulates Marjorie on bringing 'credit to our town', while a prize-winning *Mercury* journalist commends the book 'to all wives who believe that the secret of happiness in the home is crystallised in the old adage, "Feed the brute"'.

Given the genesis of the book, it's not surprising that there is a section devoted to 'Hints for Show Cooks (Given me by Show Judges)'. The aphorisms Marjorie has scattered through this part of the book suggest a theme. They include: 'Love your enemy, it'll drive him crazy', 'Envy poisons joy. How true!', 'Envy is a kind of praise' and 'Nothing is impossible, but some people are.' In accordance with Marjorie's interests, there are also sections devoted to the story of Mother's Day and the origins of Valentine's Day—with recipes for a punch called 'Loving Cups', a 'Passion Flummery', and a gelatinous mould of tomato juice, luncheon meat and hard-boiled eggs called a 'Sweetheart Shape'.

'Breakfast and luncheon dishes,' Marjorie notes in her fore-word, 'seem always to be a problem with young housewives. I hope they will find some of the answers to their problems here.' Her breakfast suggestions include kidneys on toast, lambs fry, curried eggs, scrambled brains, rabbit paste, and a simple dish ('that acts as a mild laxative as well') combining soaked rolled oats, apples, condensed milk and lemon or orange juice. Marjorie's luncheon menus are similarly hearty: lamb and broad bean casserole, bacon pudding with mustard sauce, camp pie, tongue and potato pie, tripe fritters, devilled tripe, pigeon pie with mushrooms, venison patties, and the unusual-sounding lettuce fritters.

The many recipes in *Marjorie Blackwell at Home* rely upon a relatively narrow selection of ingredients, with pantry staples to the fore. Influenced by the privations of Marjorie's childhood, the book places a strong emphasis on thrift and household management. The almost incomprehensible number of recipes for sauces, jams, chutneys, pickles, jellies and marmalades evidences the need to find ways of preserving large quantities of seasonal produce for use throughout the year. Marjorie includes a lot of 'economy' recipes designed to save on eggs, sugar and butter, and provides instructions for concocting 'mock' foods. The key ingredients of her Mock Chicken Roll are breadcrumbs and finely minced rabbit and bacon, while her Mock Ham is fashioned from a leg of lamb pumped with brine, boiled, then soused in fruit juice, crumbed and studded with cloves. Mock Crab is made out of grated and seasoned raw potato mixed with beaten egg and deep-fried, while a Mock Turkey sandwich filling is contrived from making a sauce out of butter, eggs, parsley, grated onion and herbs. Marjorie lists at least six ways of making Mock Cream, while her Substitute Butter recipe is based on beef suet and milk. She supplies two other methods for stretching butter ('for use at kitchen teas, balls, etc.'): one that involves beating it with salt and alternating dashes of hot and cold water, and another that adds milk, milk powder and gelatine.

In its emphasis on locality and seasonality, Marjorie's 1960s food philosophy resembles the one towards which many contemporary foodies are now attempting to shepherd the masses. Marjorie's audience, though, had little option but to eat local and seasonal foods. Her recipes' ingredients tell an almost forgotten tale of the changes to the availability, price and popularity of certain types of produce, meat and seafood. Her recipes for grilled wattlebird, pigeon and deer sound positively exotic to the average contemporary

Marjorie regards multitasking as one of her foremost skills.

cook; the number of dishes using brains, tripe, tongue, kidney and liver show a much greater acceptance of the need to get value out of every part of a slaughtered beast. Neither Marjorie's rabbit nor scallop dishes would in 1960s Tasmania have been expensive to prepare, but these days the quantities of these ingredients that her recipes call for are almost luxuriant.

Not surprisingly, the style of Marjorie's 1960s cuisine betrays the stodgy legacy of English cookery, yet within the pages of her first book are also little hints of the changes occurring in basic Australian home cooking. Included is an 'Italian Egg Dish' (onion, tomato, cheese, egg yolks and seasoning, served on toast), a macaroni dish, and a 'Spaghetti' in which the almost-cooked pasta is pan-fried with peeled and sliced tomatoes, and sprinkled with paprika and grated cheese.

As Marjorie says in her foreword, it was her hope that housewives would reach for her volume not only when cooking but also when 'relaxing'. A section titled 'Some of my Favourite Poems etc., I have taken from the many scrap books I have made' is a compendium of personal favourite verses, homilies, quotations and mock recipes ('4 pounds of love, half a pound of buttered youth, half a pound good looks . . .'). Here, most especially, Marjorie wears her heart on her sleeve, providing readers with insight into her deepest yearnings. She names a verse called 'More and More' and a song titled 'More' as firm favourites. She has even written some of the poetry herself, including 'Things I Love (Composed by myself)', 'My Dislikes—by me' and the acrostic paean 'Campbell Town—by me'. Verse by Browning ('Rabbi ben Ezra')

Cock Crowing
Prevent them crowing in early morning by suspending loosely a small lath above the perch, so that when he stretches his neck to crow, his comb will come gently in contact with it. This will soon stop his noise.

and Kipling ('If') is included in Marjorie's greatest hits, but of the two only Browning merits an attribution.

The topics covered in this section of the book include motherhood, ageing, Christian conduct, the sanctity of the home and the glory of the garden, but by far the most prevalent theme is romantic love. Under the heading 'Happiness No. 1', Marjorie repeats a message that she says was written in her 'favourite Christmas card in 1963':

Love cure: Recommended to take 12 oz of dislike, 1 lb. resolution, 2 oz. of the power of experience, a large sprig of time, 1 quart of the cooling water of consideration, set them over a gentle fire of love, sweetened with the sugar of forgetfulness, skim it with the spoon of melancholy, place it at the bottom of your heart, cork it with sound conscience, let it remain and you will instantly find cure to be restored to your right senses.

'If there are varieties (as of Melody) between one erotic occasion and another, a man can always enjoy HAPPINESS with one and the same woman.' But who can have penned, or quoted, such a saucy sentiment? Surely not Cliff. Perhaps 'Happiness No. 1' is one of the book's few signs that in the early 1960s Mrs Blackwell had something cooking in the romance department.

———————

Marjorie met Adrian Harry Campbell Cooper in early 1962, as she was approaching her forty-fifth birthday and when her marriage was in its twenty-fourth year. She first set eyes on the married father of five at a dance that may even have been a Valentine's Day affair. Marjorie had arrived early at the dance hall—without Cliff, as usual—having been given a lift by a friend who was the pianist for the night. She recalls:

> The first two to arrive at the dance were Adrian and his wife . . . Adrian
> was saddled with a rug, and a radiator that was plugged into the power
> point behind the column in the hall. Then he would carefully wrap the
> rug around his wife and I often said, 'Oh, what a sissy!'

Five years Marjorie's senior, Adrian had been raised in Adelaide
before moving to Tasmania in his twenties to work as a Congregational Church pastor. By the time he and Marjorie met,
Adrian had long given up preaching in favour of school teaching.
He had moved around various country schools and now had been
posted to Campbell Town. Courteous and educated, religious and
romantic, Adrian Cooper was—to Marjorie—everything Cliff
Blackwell was not.

In the 'ABC of Happy Marriage' in *Marjorie Blackwell at Home*,
A is for 'ALWAYS: No refunds if not satisfied, so choose carefully.'
Doubtless this was an ideal that she held dear, and one she attempted
to instil in her sons. But she may not have foreseen how dissatisfied
one could become with a spouse, nor how appealing might be a
replacement model. At first-aid training sessions in early 1962 an
attraction sparked between Marjorie and Adrian. It was kindled when
each of them signed up to volunteer for the newly formed Campbell
Town division of St John Ambulance and began travelling around
the state to various events, away from their respective spouses.

> I started to grow extremely fond of Adrian, but neither of us thought
> anything would come of it as I had said many a time that the man who
> could lure me away from 'Climar' would have to be a saint (and later
> I found out he was). We often said we would wait for one another so
> no-one would be hurt, even if it meant waiting nearly for ever.

But the pair did not wait forever. By October 1964 Adrian had left
his wife, and though Marjorie clung to her life at Climar for a further

Marjorie Blackwell and Adrian Cooper were thrown together in the early 1960s, when they both joined the new Campbell Town chapter of St John Ambulance.

fourteen tempestuous months, for all of that time it was Adrian who was first and foremost in her thoughts.

⟶⟶◆◆⟵

From adolescence Marjorie has kept a record of her daily doings. Though her early diaries have been lost, those dating from January 1, 1964 to December 31, 2006 have survived and are remarkably complete. In the pages of commercially produced diaries ranging from pocket to letter-sized, these four decades of Marjorie's busy years have been meticulously accounted for. Where there are empty pages in the diaries it is usually because Marjorie has gone on holidays and kept her record in separate travel journals. The length of her entries varies from year to year, depending on the dimensions and layout of the books themselves. Where the books allow for half a

AT one time I wrote the following and left it lying about in the home hoping it would be read. I still have it. Here is part of what I wrote:–
"I wish I could start this with why I love my Husband, but I can't, because of how you treat me mentally and physically, so I'd be lying and cheating. When you are kind to me you are tops, but when you are not curbing your language and threatening me, I detest you. Treat me right, and you know I return it, treat me wrong, and I cannot return it, as my upbringing has been different. I forgive you so easily, which is my greatest downfall and the reason I guess why I stay in my haven. You can be perfect when you like, then I admire you, but that urge to hurt comes too often. Then (the thing I loathe most) you tell the first person you meet – be he rich man or beggar – about our arguments, home life, and worse still, lies that grow bigger from house to house. After you have gossiped and lied to all and sundry, you often return home, see me upset and declare you won't do it again. I disliked you immensely when you had the telephone cut off so I couldn't ring news through to the press or A.B.C. as you know perfectly well I reversed the charges, but when I had it put back on in my name, you used it and let me foot the bill. I loved you for letting me have the privilege of designing our new home 'Climar', the fence and the gates, and thanks for buying the contents of some rooms. I love you for helping me wash up when I am busy with show cooking . . . Our sexual relations are perfect – I wish for nothing better – but I do not like forced sex when you are in a temper, or the times when you commence, then stop, just to make me angry. I dislike you when you humiliate me in front of people, using bad language in front of our children, and the stupid things you do when you are annoyed. You make me suffer mentally, although I am always striving to do my best. I do your bookwork, manage your affairs, use my savings to keep you out of debt, cook you nourishing meals, do your mending, make your clothes, do the garden, inside and outside work, and have practically reared the boys as you are never here. What else can I do?"

CAUSES OF FAILURE IN JAM

If jam becomes mouldy . . .
- it was insufficiently boiled;
- sealed before allowed to cool;
- stored in a warm place.

If jam does not set . . .
- the fruit was over-ripe;
- excessive water used;
- jam was under-boiled.

If jam crystallises . . .
- it was over-boiled;
- excessive sugar used.

page per day, she has written half a page; where the books offer a full page, a full page she has duly filled.

Though Marjorie's own emotions and the progress of her affairs of the heart feature prominently in her writings, she also used her diary for pragmatic purposes, such as to keep track of gifts given and received, to note important correspondence, to keep tabs on her health problems and periods, and to account for her use of time. Frequently, sentences relating to a number of these purposes will be sandwiched in a single entry, such as this one from June 6, 1964: 'Husband angry. Saw accident. Car upside down in water. Cooked sultana cake, rock cakes, meringues, Anzacs & shortbread for show. Doing stupid things. Left sugar out of Anzacs, etc. Lonely day. Music playing. Memories.'

Written in cramped, looping cursive in the top band of a five-year pocket-sized diary, Marjorie's entries for 1964 chart a dissolving marriage and a burgeoning love affair. It was a year when Cliff was frequently away from home, and Marjorie's moods see-sawed in accordance with his presences and absences. Throughout the

FLUFFED EGGS

Stiffly beat 4 egg whites with salt and pepper. Pile on to buttered toast. Drop yolks into each hollowed centre. Draw the egg-white over the top. Sprinkle with grated cheese if liked and bake in a moderate oven until egg is set.

RABBIT PASTE

2 rabbits, 1 lb. bacon, ½ lb. butter, 3 tablespoons anchovy sauce.

Cut rabbits into pieces. Put in basin with butter and bacon. Steam 4 hours, when meat should be tender. Mince twice, add juice, and anchovy sauce. Reheat, but do not boil. Put in jars and seal. Serve on toast for breakfast or lunch.

LETTUCE FRITTERS

These are delicious and are excellent for that Saturday night tea, or any, for that matter. Makes a nice meal for a family of four.

1 heart of a lettuce, 1 onion, 1 egg, fat, S.R. [self-rising] **flour, pepper and salt.**

Shred lettuce finely, add grated onion, beaten egg, salt and pepper to taste. Mix well. Add enough S.R. flour to make a good stiff batter. Drop by tablespoon into hot fat and cook on both sides until well browned. Serve at once.

MARJORIE'S CAKE

A very delicious and unusual cake and one of my favourites.

Cake mixture: 2 eggs, 1 small cup sugar, ½ cup butter, 1 small cup milk, 1 cup S.R. flour.

Pastry mixture: 1½ cups S.R. flour, ½ cup butter, ¼ cup milk.

Rub the butter into the flour until there are no lumps. Add milk and mix to a soft dough. Roll out and line a square cake tin 7 in. x 7 in. Spread with raspberry or plum jam, then sprinkle with 1 cup of currants. Make sponge by putting all ingredients in a bowl (butter melted) and beat vigorously for 3 minutes. Pour into pastry case over currants, etc. Bake in moderate oven 1 hour. Ice when cold with plain icing.

PIGEON PIE WITH MUSHROOMS

Clean 3 young pigeons, cut off the feet and wrap each bird in a slice of fat bacon. At the bottom of a pie dish put ½ lb. rump steak, cut into thin slices. Place the pigeons, breast upward on this, and pack mushrooms around. Season, then add ¼ pint water. Cover with puff pastry, decorate with pastry leaves and brush with beaten egg; bake in a fairly hot oven for 1½ hours. Add some hot stock before serving. Serve with creamed potatoes.

CLIFF'S CAKE

4 oz. butter, 5 oz. castor sugar (1 oz. sprinkled on top afterwards), 2 ozs. flour, 4 ozs. cornflour, 1 level teaspoon baking powder, pinch salt, 2 eggs, vanilla essence, 1 tablespoon milk.

Cream the butter and 4 ozs. sugar until soft and fluffy. Sift dry ingredients. Add eggs one at a time and 1 tablespoon of sifted flour with each egg to prevent it curdling. Fold in rest of flour, vanilla essence and milk and bake in a moderate oven for 1 hour, after dusting the top of cake with the remaining 1 oz. castor sugar.

SPONGE CAKE PRIZE
(No rising)

This is my husband's favourite cake – a cake that I have never been beaten with, in competitive work.

4 eggs, 1 level cup sugar, pinch salt, 1 rounded cup plain flour, 1 teaspoon lemon juice.

Grease a square tin, then dust out with plain flour or icing sugar. Separate yolks from the whites of the eggs. Beat yolks and sugar together until creamy (about 3 minutes with an electric beater). Beat whites a little before adding salt, then beat till a stiff froth. Now add both together, and beat about 10 minutes. It should be thick and creamy. Fold in the plain flour (sifted), then the lemon juice. Bake 1 hour in a very moderate oven to cook it well. If the oven is too hot, the sponge will rise in the centre and crack, or if, on the other hand, the oven is too slow, the cake will be sticky underneath and on top.

HIS WIFE

You're the mother who bears him his children;
You're the nurse when he's worn out and ill;
You're the hand in his hand when he's lonely;
You're the star shining over Life's Hill;
You're the strength of his home when he's
    worried;
You're his solace when things go all wrong;
You're the listener to all his worries;
You're the laughter that gives Life its song;
You're the comforter in his despairing;
You're the sharer throughout all his life;
You're the girl whom he ardently married;
You're his woman, his love, and his life.

year she records 'filthy language', 'tongue pie', 'vile talk', 'dirty talk', 'awful abusive language', 'big row', 'merry hell', 'hell of a blue' and 'horrible things said'. While there are occasional entries along the lines of 'Husband exceptionally nice, as can be', 'Cliff nice to me', 'No swearing, growling, etc.', she more often records feeling 'lonely', 'frustrated', 'discontented', 'sick of him' and 'fed up'.

Adrian's presence is everywhere in the 1964 entries, though often coded, no doubt because of Marjorie's fear that her diary would be discovered and read by Cliff. A small symbol, sometimes resembling an eye and other times looking more like a rectangle with a dot in the centre, accompanies many of Marjorie's more joyous days; 'x-----x' is another common cipher; the phrase 'fed the fowls' seems to carry more significance than might be expected. For August 31, 1964, a day when Cliff was away, Marjorie notes: 'Washing. Prepared for

Anne. Arrived at 9 o'clock & stayed for 27 hours.' For Anne, read Adrian—in other documents Marjorie recorded that '27 hours of heaven' with Adrian began on this date.

The 1964 diary also records Marjorie's anxious dependence on the mail, which is unsurprising given that during this period 'Marjorie wrote 534 pages (love letters) to Adrian, and Adrian 322¼ to Marjorie'. Clearly, the two were by this stage planning a future together. 'Rest assured, you fill my mind and heart at all moments of my waking life, but I hope my darling *you* don't wake me at night with the clickety clack of knitting needles from 3am,' Adrian wrote in one of his missives. And: 'I feel quite proud to think that you are mine, that I won't be under a petticoat government, and that I'll be able to do all the things that I've wanted to do without restriction.' He refers also to her 'husband's stupidity', sympathises that 'You have missed so much of what you want out of life,' and promises that he will place her upon her rightful pedestal. We can only imagine the speed and intensity of the gossip that must have been sweeping up and down Campbell Town's main street.

(from) *To Do with Clothes*

==> Give an extra touch of glamour to your black evening shoes by adding a pair of your clip-on glittering ear rings.

==> If your evening shoes are shabby, paint with liquid glue or nail varnish and sprinkle with gold or silver glitter while wet.

==> Re-stiffen your nylon petticoat after washing by adding a packet of gelatine to 1 gallon of water, and rinse garment thoroughly in it. Dry over an open umbrella. A tablespoon of white sugar to a pint of warm water is also good.

==> Paint your jewellery with nail polish, and the stones won't fall out.

==> One aspirin crushed and soaked with perspiry articles will take out all odour and stains as well.

In her autobiography Marjorie writes that November 11, 1964, was the last night she slept at Climar, 'because of what sometimes went on in my bed'. The reader is left to guess what Marjorie means by this, but her diary entry for the date is chilling in its bluntness: 'Did Mrs Jones skirt. Made the roses for my frock. Spring cleaned two porches. Made petticoat for my dress. Cliff home. Raped me at night & tore the sheet doing it.' Attached to this entry there is, in different ink, a presumably retrospective addition: 'His last one.' And in other documentation Marjorie has noted against the date November 11, 1964: 'Ex-husband raped me for the last time.'

Life Is for Living states that this night was Marjorie's last at Climar, and that for a further thirteen months she occupied the house only in daylight hours. Her pattern was to spend days at the house engaged in her usual chores, and then to sleep at a friend's place. Presumably, this arrangement was her way of avoiding the violence, while retaining a claim on the house during the final disintegration of her marriage. Her diaries reveal, however, that she did sometimes sleep at Climar during those months, perhaps only risking it when she knew Cliff was away.

Though Marjorie's accounts seem to add up to an allegation that the November 11 episode was far from an isolated event, that date was nevertheless a turning point. The next day Cliff had Marjorie's name removed from their joint cheques, so he must have been aware that a split was imminent. Marjorie was experienced at keeping up appearances, and within days she was in sufficiently good form to proudly host an overnight visit from the reigning Miss Tasmania, begin her career as a judge on the show circuit, and make for her grandson's birthday the intricate train cake pictured in the pages of *Marjorie Blackwell at Home*.

Although 1965 brought Marjorie the excitement of her first book's publication, it was otherwise a turbulent and difficult year. In the

Marjorie hand-feeds one of her many pets, an orphaned joey, at Campbell Town.

PICKLED ONIONS No. 1
My Prize Recipe

This method helps to preserve whiteness of onions.
Small pickling onions, brine, milk, 1 quart spiced vinegar.

Remove outer skins and soak the onions in strong brine made with ¼ lb. salt to 1 quart water. Onions should be well covered with the brine and left soaking for 3 days, changing the brine every day. At the end of 3 days drain well and wipe each onion dry. Place in a basin. Bring to the boil equal parts of milk and water and pour it over the onions, completely covering them. Allow to become cold, drain, and again wipe each onion dry, cover with spiced vinegar, cover down air tight.

Spiced Vinegar:

3 pints vinegar (white preferred), 1 teaspoon cloves, 1 tablespoon bruised ginger, 1 tablespoon peppercorns, 1 clove minced garlic, 2 blades mace, ½ cup sugar, 2 teaspoons salt.

Place all in saucepan and bring to boiling point, simmer 15 minutes. Cover and stand aside until cold. Strain and use.

sepia-toned photograph that graces the cover of *Marjorie Blackwell at Home* our heroine stands—chest-puffingly proud—in front of Climar, wearing her Sunday best of gathered-waist frock, white bucket-shaped hat and white court shoes. Here, ostensibly, we see the perfect housewife, standing in front of her perfect home. But by the time the first copies of the book rolled off the presses, in April 1965, the enviable home life of Tasmania's pre-eminent housewife was nothing more than a facade. Marjorie's lover, Adrian Cooper, had at the beginning of the year been transferred from Campbell Town to a school in the south, more than an hour away by car from her and the battle she was waging. Whenever possible, Marjorie went south to spend time with him, and her diary entries for the year are littered with such snippets as 'breakfast in bed from a loved one', 'missing my baby', 'Spoilt my baby, breakfast, morning tea & dinner in bed', 'gave my darling breakfast in bed', 'Lovely evening in his arms', 'cooked, washed and ironed for my loved one', and 'Watched my beloved from the window.'

By now it was not only Cliff with whom Marjorie was in conflict; Gerald was also taking exception to his mother's obvious infidelity. Ross remained steadfast in his connection with his mother through this difficult time, but Gerald was apparently incensed. According to Marjorie, he began to return gifts and cards, and then—in May 1965—he stopped contact between her and his two sons, aged four and two. No doubt Gerald loved his father and felt injured on his behalf, but I wonder if he also felt more personally aggrieved by his mother's actions. Having been drilled in the sanctity of marriage, and having tied the knot at eighteen, how did he feel when his mother seemed to disregard that deeply held ideal?

APPLE PUDDING IN RHYME

Melt in a saucepan with due care,
A tablespoon of butter fair;
Stir it in 'till smooth it be,
Two ounces of flour – stir constantly,
Two cups of milk to it you add,
Three minutes boil or you'll be sad.
Next turn into a basin clean
And mix therein with mind serene.

> One ounce of sugar, nothing more,
> Then beat two yolks and spread them o'er
> The two whites beat to a stiff froth
> To stir together, don't be loth,
> Pour all upon a sweetened bed
> Of apples, cooked, and even spread
> Inside a baking dish, then bake –
> Just twenty minutes it should take.

There was still more grief to come for Marjorie. In her autobiography she makes sensational claims about a series of bizarre events in 1965 that finally caused her to abandon her hopes of remaining mistress of Climar. Her account reads as fiction, but each of its episodes has its uncontrived—though not always entirely congruent—counterpart in her diaries. In two separate attacks in July somebody (but not Cliff: he was away camping) savaged her garden, hacking off standard and weeping roses at their butts. Later, when Marjorie was shopping in the main streets of Hobart, the coat she was wearing began to disintegrate; likewise a dress, the following day. The damage to her garments, she writes, was done by a vandal with battery acid, though she believes that Cliff 'would never have stooped so low as to do that'.

By late August, Marjorie seems to have made up her mind to leave.

She had her sister Beatrice take away and store the most precious of their family heirlooms, and she began shifting her belongings south. During the process of packing and loading she felt that she was being watched, and she and Adrian were nearly driven off the road by another vehicle that Marjorie believes was following them with its lights off.

By September, Marjorie had more or less moved in with Adrian. The couple rather unromantically marked the beginning of their cohabitation by visiting the dogs' home to pick up a watchdog for protection. They were living, she writes, 'in seclusion', and on one occasion Marjorie found it necessary to hide while an 'inspector' came to look over Adrian's house. And all the while Marjorie was busily keeping up her public profile as the housewife with all the answers, conducting stain-removal demonstrations on Hobart's Channel Six, among other engagements.

At last Marjorie conceded, and the battle for Climar was over: 'on Tuesday the 7th December 1965, I walked slowly out the front door of "Climar" for the last time,' she records. Following Marjorie and Cliff's divorce, the home would eventually be sold and the proceeds divided. 'No one knows how I felt that evening, leaving the home I designed and half paid for, decorated and slaved in and around,' Marjorie writes. Despite her sadness, she knew that her dream home was a necessary sacrifice if she was to be successful in her new and overriding ambition: to become Mrs Adrian Cooper.

YOU want a man who loves you for what you are. Look for a man who'll bring you flowers and leave notes under the pillow. A woman can take any amount of that you know. You want a man who'll say 'that was a lovely meal', and not just wolf it down. There's no sense marrying just for sex, you've got to have someone you can sit down with, after dinner, and talk things over. When choosing a husband, find one who is always on time and keeps his promises. Note his manners when taking you on a date, and pay careful attention if he has clean shoes and wears a shirt and tie. Beware if he suddenly says (when it's time for payment) 'oh, dear, my wallet is in my other coat pocket'. Note how he treats his parents, and if he takes you on a tour of the home, notice if his room is tidy.

3

Marjorie Cooper

WHEN Marjorie compares the relative merits and demerits of her three husbands, as she does frequently in the pages of her autobiography, it is almost always Adrian Cooper who takes the cake. In Adrian, Marjorie found not only a man she could respect and adore, but also one who was prepared to supply all the surprise love notes and thoughtful gifts that her romantic heart could desire. A recurrent theme in the letters and verses that Marjorie wrote for Adrian during their brief relationship is the well-worn sentiment 'I love you not only for what you are, but for what I am when I am with you.' Loved by Adrian, Marjorie felt profoundly affirmed for the first time in her life, and it was a heady sensation. 'It was extremely hard at first to adjust to Adrian after living with such an aggravating person,' she writes in her autobiography. 'It was like being born again, once I realised it was true.'

But while there were roses galore in the Cooper marital bed, there was also the occasional thorn. 'If any one asks me now what I think about remarrying,' Marjorie writes, 'I tell them *fine*, but first find out if he has any daughters.' For although he was practically perfect in every other respect, Adrian was the father of three girls. Marjorie would eventually form a solid bond with Adrian's two sons, yet her difficulties with his daughters started early and were not easily overcome. Even during the clandestine phase of Marjorie and Adrian's love affair, in the months prior to Marjorie's final departure from Climar, grievances were being notched up between Marjorie and the young women who would eventually become her stepdaughters. In a letter Marjorie discovered, she found herself described by one of the girls as 'a common type' who was simply 'using' Adrian. It was a barb that stung, and the injury took Marjorie a long time to forgive.

Marjorie seems to have expected that Adrian's daughters would unquestioningly embrace her as a fixture in their lives, even though she must have known that they regarded her as the chief architect of their parents' separation, and even though she must have understood the concerns they held for their jilted mother. Still, she didn't seem to cut them much slack during the time when they were adjusting to a radical alteration to their family's shape. She complains: 'If he wasn't receiving letters, it was phone calls for money, or visits would be made with me entirely ignored, and presents given to try to hurt me—such as an ashtray, because he gave up smoking for me.'

The way Marjorie saw it, her position at Adrian's side automatically entitled her to respect, inclusion and deference from his children. After all, she wouldn't have tolerated anything less from her sons in their dealings with Adrian. In her world, romantic love trumps filial devotion every time.

EYEBROW LINER MISSING? Don't worry. Take a match, the bigger the better. Burn tip of it until black, then let it cool off. You can use it on your eyebrows like a pencil liner.

ROUGE: If you are out of rouge, cut a beet in half and use cut side on your cheeks.

Trying simultaneously to please his new lover and to reassure his daughters of his ongoing affection and commitment, Adrian must have been in a tight spot. 'His children come first. That's all I get,' Marjorie laments in one diary entry, late in 1965. And, in another: 'I honestly wanted to end it all, so as [I] wouldn't be in the way of . . . him from going to see his children every two weeks. They are his whole life, but I'm not their mother, so don't fit in.' But before long, her fighting spirit had returned: 'I'm not taking 2nd place to his family,' she wrote early in 1966, the year she would cement her claim with wedding vows.

At the beginning of 1966 Marjorie and Adrian put some distance between themselves and their families, moving to the township of Redpa, in Tasmania's far north-west. Here, Adrian was to take up the post of headmaster at the local school. Redpa is a windswept agricultural outpost that many Tasmanians would struggle to pinpoint on a map. On the day Marjorie and Adrian drove the long twisting road from Hobart to Redpa, with their trusty caravan in tow, it seemed that the journey would last forever. When finally they approached the township, Marjorie felt as if they had 'come to the end of the world'.

Since the community expected faultless moral standards from its new headmaster, Adrian could hardly be seen to be living with a woman to whom he was not married. So Marjorie once again embarked on a double life, acting as housewife in the labyrinthine thirteen-room house in which Adrian was accommodated, but ostensibly boarding with the family who lived next door. It must have been déjà-vu for Marjorie to cook and clean and play house at one abode while sleeping nights at another.

Despite her fractured living arrangements, Marjorie threw herself with her usual gusto into the project of constructing a new life. Soon she and Adrian had infiltrated every aspect of community activity. They busied themselves with overhauling the school's gardens, attending the committee meetings for the local fire brigade, progress association, and parents and friends. There were also parties, cabarets, church, polling station duties, debutante balls and dances, with Adrian frequently the master of ceremonies. Progressive dinners were popular and 'Tupper parties were raging,' Marjorie remembers. On the up-to-the-minute Singer that Adrian bought her, Marjorie zipped up dresses and costumes for her new circle of friends and neighbours, all the while keeping up her correspondence work for Tasmania's northern newspapers, the *Examiner* and the *Advocate*, and also for the ABC. Adrian joined the cricket and football clubs (Marjorie sat on the ladies committee), and—while there was no local CWA branch for Marjorie to join—there was the Redpa Show. When Marjorie blazed onto the scene in 1966, forty of the sixty items she entered won prizes. Naturally,

FLOWERS LASTING LONGER IN VASES

Flowers with milky fluid in their stems will wilt immediately if you do not sear the stem tips with a flame. Scrape other stems to allow the maximum to be absorbed. If stems are thick, split them from the base for several centimetres. Freshly cut stems absorb more water, so cut the stem with a sharp knife or secateurs. Strip all leaves which will be under water. They will quickly decay if you don't and make the water smelly. Always use water at room temperature, so have the vase filled the night before with water, to make sure of this. Always clean vases thoroughly and rinse with boiling water to remove soap and eliminate bacteria. Flowers keep fresh longer in a vase if they are in a tea made from foxglove flowers – or 2 tablespoons of white vinegar and 2 teaspoons sugar in a litre of water. Don't leave flowers in a stuffy or draughty location. Keep them away from fireplaces, radiators or direct sunlight.

she also took home the trophy for the most successful exhibitor.

Engaged in home-making and contributing to community life, Marjorie was in her element. The Tupperware parties she hosted were successful, she started driving lessons, and her beloved Adrian remembered her forty-ninth birthday with a brand new Electrolux. Though one of Adrian's daughters came to stay for Easter and Marjorie felt relegated to the 'background' during the visit, she confidently entered in her diary that this would be 'the last time'. By the middle of 1966 both Marjorie's and Adrian's divorces had been granted, and financial scores had been settled with both former spouses. To Marjorie's delight, she was now free to send out wedding invitations.

Though Marjorie, in her autobiography, recalls her wedding preparations as 'joyous', her diaries tell a slightly different story. In the months leading up to the big day Marjorie was frequently ill, stressed and at odds with her intended. One diary entry, written after a social event that went badly, reveals a fracture in Marjorie's usual self-assurance:

> One of my darling's favourite sayings was 'If winter comes – can spring be far behind?'

> I don't fit because I can't talk about the things he likes, as I am not intelligent enough, but he should be able to join in with my small talk. Where will it end. I've never felt so inferior as I feel today. All that remains is for me to be a good housewife.

This last comment is unprecedentedly negative about the status of domestic work—perhaps indicating the intensity of the emotions that Marjorie was experiencing during this difficult time. She was struggling with the fact that some people disapproved of her remarrying. Most hurtfully, she received 'a most uncalled for insulting lunatic of a letter from Doreen', her older sister, who at the eleventh hour pulled out of the role of matron of honour. Her younger sister, Beatrice, quickly filled the void.

———

Every detail of Marjorie and Adrian's nuptials is recorded in *Our Wedding Book*, a cream-jacketed volume with pages edged by generic bridal-themed illustrations in fetching shades of fuchsia and teal. Beneath such titles as 'The Story of Our Romance', 'Trousseau', 'Guests', 'Gifts', 'Homecoming', 'Our First Home' and 'We Entertain' are blank spaces for a dutiful bride to fill in. Marjorie has crammed

Sometimes [Cliff] would forget the detergent altogether. Adrian was sparing when he did [the washing up], and Eric is heavy handed and likes cool water.

Cliff was not the least bit interested in my first book, Adrian read it from cover to cover and Eric does not read much so does not know the contents of any.

Cliff was always noisy, even with walking, and his high pitched voice told you when he was about. Adrian's voice was clear and distinct, but Eric has a low, soft voice and does not open his mouth very wide, so quite often I do not catch what he says.

[Adrian] was very quick in his actions (Cliff strode about as if he didn't have a minute to spare, and Eric is just the opposite).

Adrian always controlled his temper because he used to say that anger was a short madness, but this day he lost it for a second he was so hurt. (Cliff had a violent temper, Eric a quick one, but he is soon over it.)

Clifford . . . means "brave" (he certainly was). Adrian's name means "pessimistic and hard to please" and Eric's name means "like a prince".

Marjorie's favourite picture of her second husband, Adrian Cooper, taken during a holiday to his home state of South Australia.

her memento book with newspaper clippings, photographs and her own thorough recollections. In best newspaper columnist style Marjorie describes the bridal outfit she made:

> Material was of exclusive blue ribboned lace, lined with blue taffeta. The frock was short, with scalloped hem, and also scalloped on the edge of short sleeves and square neck. It was finished with a bow on [the] waistline, and pearls adorned the bodice. A fascinator to match was worn on the hair. Long white gloves and white lace nylon shoes completed the ensemble. The trailing bouquet was of artificial white satin roses, blue forget-me-nots and hyacinths, finished with blue and white satin ribbon.

Taped securely into the book is a swatch of the blue-ribboned lace, along with a square of the bone-coloured Airtex fabric from which, Marjorie records, she made a pair of shortie pyjamas for Adrian to wear on the honeymoon. The trousseau was kept to a minimum, she says, because the honeymoon was to be spent mostly in a caravan. Nevertheless, on the 'Trousseau' page she details the fabric and design of the three fancy nightgowns she packed in anticipation of her first nights of wedded bliss. She also describes the matching handmade his 'n' hers outfits that the couple wore through the honeymoon, eliciting 'many a stir and glance': the 'sweaters—royal blue & grey—were made by the bride, and the trousers (his) and skirt (hers) were of steel grey melange'.

A highlight of the wedding book is Marjorie's account, in verse, of the preparations:

> Our engagement lasted for just a month,
> For wedding invitations and replies,
> And planning and making the famous dress,
> Oh dear me, how the time flies.

The day started right on the 26th,
With Adrian and Maggie to tea,
Then as the days followed the air grew tense,
With refusals from loved ones you see.

Ringing and writing and thinking up names,
Packing and sewing and spending,
Depressed the best part of me some of the days.
My shattered old nerves needed mending.

Then came replies from our truest friends,
'Yes for sure we'll be there,' they said,
And presents and cards from others that couldn't,
Showed us how well they were bred.

Making my wedding cake gave me a thrill
As did the bouquets and headgear,
Not to mention the attendant's frock,
That I made when feeling so queer.

Continuing for a further four stanzas, the poem relates the characteristically dramatic events that unfolded as the wedding day drew near.

Five days before the wedding a legal obstacle cropped up. Marjorie and Adrian's lawyer phoned to say that the ceremony might have to be postponed: Cliff had failed to sign one last, crucial document relating to his divorce from Marjorie. Though the legality of the impending marriage was now in doubt, Marjorie and Adrian made their way to Hobart, where the August 27 wedding was scheduled to take place in the Memorial Congregational Church, not far from the city centre. It was the day before the wedding when the despondent couple once again heard from their legal representatives, but this time 'it was Reginald Wright (now Sir) speaking, not the

Dog's Coat
Make from the sleeve of a discarded sweater. Cut holes for armholes.

son.' 'Be at the courtroom at two this afternoon,' Wright senior said, and duly he set matters straight. But there was more to come: 'To top it all up,' Marjorie writes, 'we were told that there was going to be a scene at the church next day by Cliff, so we had plain clothes policemen dotted about, just in case.'

If there was a plot to disrupt the wedding, it did not eventuate. Instead, the ceremony was the flawless realisation of 49-year-old Marjorie's long-held romantic fantasies:

The Coopers on their wedding day, in 1966. Marjorie made the cake herself, at Redpa, and packed it in a suitcase to take it to the wedding in Hobart.

> When I entered the church, and the organ was playing 'Here comes the bride', I became overwhelmed when Adrian turned around and faced me as I made my way with trembling knees up the aisle on the arm of Ross. But Adrian's face was beaming. He had been waiting for this moment for so long, and I'd always wanted a church wedding, pretty frock, guests and breakfast—what woman doesn't?—and now I had them all.

The couple's wedding breakfast was held at Newlands House, Lenah Valley, and their wedding night at the Jason Motor Inn, Lindisfarne. At the end of a caravanning honeymoon Mr and Mrs Cooper returned to Redpa, where they were now at liberty to share a home. Marjorie recalls: 'Adrian carried me over the thresh-hold, and after a "cuppa", christened the Queen Anne bed that had been made up for eight months. It was heavenly to be as one.'

Marjorie had endured the tumult of her separation from Cliff, and the insecurity of the months leading up to her wedding. But now, with her connection to Adrian confirmed in law, she entered a calmer, more positive phase of her life. When she attended a dance on the north-west coast in all the splendour of her ribboned lace wedding dress, she was voted Ballerina of the Ball. This small triumph was followed by a period of house hunting in Devonport, where Adrian and Marjorie had set their sights on living. By October 1966 they had settled on a modest brick bungalow on a bare block in Madden Street, installing tenants there until Adrian could secure a transfer and they could move in themselves.

In January 1967 the Coopers came as close as they ever would to joint parenthood when Adrian bought for Marjorie the little white poodle pup that would be her companion for nearly two decades. She was christened Freda Fi Fi, the 'Freda' part a nod to Marjorie's first middle name, Alfreda. (There was also a lamb named Willis, after Marjorie's second middle name.) 'Adrian went into raptures over that dog,' Marjorie recalls. He made a special indoor bed for Freda and arranged for an expensive outdoor kennel, while Marjorie made her coats and ordered little booties for her to wear outside, so her paws would be clean when she came indoors. Each year she had her own little birthday party of sorts, and was fed patty cakes, ice-cream and a chocolate frog.

Marriage had a steadying effect upon Marjorie, yet the late 1960s was not a period of great progress in her public or publishing activity. Though she continued to contribute recipes to various publications and took on a new

Gift for a Wedding

When writing the greeting card to go with the gift, write the description of the gift on the opposite page. This will help the person setting out the gifts (for display) and later, the bride when she writes thank you notes.

Weight Watching

If you take 2 teaspoons gelatine in chilled fruit juice, half an hour before a meal, you will find it a superb appetite depressant. Gelatine does not actually make you lose weight, but because of its high protein content it has a satisfying effect on a large appetite and so weight is lost due to the smaller intake of food.

role as a social correspondent for the *Advocate*, she focused on being a wife and homemaker. When Adrian was appointed headmaster at a school at Spreyton, he and Marjorie left Redpa behind and moved to Madden Street, where the undeveloped house and garden were an inviting prospect for such keen renovators. When the Coopers moved in at Christmas, 1967, they christened their new home 'Mar-ian'—first three letters of Marjorie, last three letters of Adrian—and began transforming the property into something uniquely their own.

Marjorie and Adrian dug up all the plants they had grown and nurtured in Redpa, and potted them in jars and tins collected from the dump. It took several trips to transport them by caravan to Madden Street, where Marjorie had to fight the unyielding soil. She had always taken an interest in plants, and now became passionate about her garden. Marjorie pored through catalogues for unusual plants, mail-ordering specimens by the hundreds. Meanwhile, she and Adrian set to work making paths, rockeries, a birdbath, fishpond, chook house [hen-house] and compost bins—'as we were determined to alter the structure of the soil'.

> As time went on I became more greedy for flowers and less lawn and Adrian never knew what to expect when he came home from school. In fact I dug up that much of the back lawn for flower beds that he erected a cyclone fence around what was left, to stop me . . . Sometimes, when he walked in, he would say 'Where's that shrub from the front lawn?' and I would say, 'Oh, I shifted that today to around the back'—and I am afraid that is still going on. I am 'Mrs Shift-It'. It's a disease.

Gerald and his children were still absent from Marjorie's life but Ross visited regularly, and on Marjorie and Adrian's second wedding anniversary he announced he was to marry his sweetheart. Before long Marjorie would once again enjoy having grandchildren. Her garden was flourishing, and Mar-ian was resplendent with the addition of a porch featuring arching panels of red, royal blue and bright yellow glass, as well as a clear panel featuring a sandblasted design selected by Adrian: 'a lady in an evening dress coming down a stairway to the waiting arms of her lover, and the word "Mar-ian" . . . written underneath'.

Gown Protected

If you live in the country and walk to parties or dances, protect the bottom of your frock with a rubbish bag. Make 2 leg holes and pull on up to waist. It may look strange, but your frock will keep clean.

In 1969 Marjorie was excited to learn that she had been selected to appear on a Melbourne-produced television game show hosted by Mike Preston. It was fortunate that Adrian accompanied her to Melbourne and to the television studio, because she had an attack of shyness when it was her turn to spin the wheel and Adrian had to step in, his spin netting a deluxe Gasglo heater.

Times were good for Marjorie and Adrian. For a while, the greatest problem Marjorie faced was a case of tennis elbow caused by too much knitting. But summer's lease had all too short a date.

In early 1970 Marjorie watched with concern as Adrian set down his tools in the middle of a painting job and sat for half an hour on the garden path. Marjorie herself was unwell at the time, suffering from a large gallstone. She was admitted to hospital for surgery and, during the first few days of her stay, Adrian was as attentive as usual,

What Is a Husband? (my version)

A good husband is a man who treats a wife as if he isn't married to her. There is a particular brand of togetherness with husbands that you can never feel with anyone else. He is simply all the good things in life wrapped up in one, a lovely warm person – either small, medium or large sized. A husband is a man who understands you and loves you for the way you are, and not for the way he would like you to be. A husband is a man with whom to share a quarrel, with no hard feelings afterwards. A husband is a man who halves all your troubles and doubles all your pleasures just by being around when they happen. A husband has to be crafty enough to outwit women, but not silly enough to think they don't know it. A husband is a man who says "we", not "I". A husband is someone you cannot hurt without hurting yourself, who brings you the first rose from the garden, rubs your back, praises your meals, mows the lawns and chops the wood. A husband is someone who wakes you up when the baby is crying, hangs around hungrily when a meal is cooking – then disappears when it is served. A husband is a lover who never has to go home, or who never feels too old to hold hands or say "I love you". A husband is someone who forgets your birthday, forgets your anniversary, but also forgets your grey hairs and wrinkles. A husband is someone whose Christmas card takes 20 minutes longer to choose than anyone else's because the words never mean enough. A husband is someone who will watch cricket, football or cartoons on the T.V. all day, but finds a job when news or something educational comes on. A husband is the one you hope to die before – so that you are never left without him.

Husbands don't like yapping dogs, cats on the garden, wearing ties, shaving at weekends, women drivers, other people's children, going shopping and visiting. Husbands like Saturdays, football, cricket, T.V. fights, camping out, fishing, cars, rare steaks, looking at girls, talking, workshops, machinery that can be taken apart, very old clothes, poking the fire, apple pie, horses and big dogs. He's happiest when taking something apart; saddest when his wife repairs something he gave up on; slowest when she is liveliest; and maddest waiting outside a shop that his wife is in.

Marjorie whipped up this frock out of Patons Totem in the early 1940s, along with a matching leggings-suit for baby Gerald.

Cliff and Marjorie Blackwell in the very early, and best, days of their marriage.

Marjorie Blackwell, resplendent in her 1950s dancing attire.

Marjorie's 1955 Campbell Town dream home, Climar, as it is today. The name is a combination of the first three letters of Cliff's and Marjorie's names.

163 Madden Street, Devonport, as it was in the 1970s, featuring the multicoloured triple-arched porch added by Marjorie and Adrian.

Marjorie, with Freda Fi Fi at heel, crosses the replica Batman Bridge that in the 1970s became a feature of her Devonport backyard. The concrete pond represents the Tamar River, and miniature picnic tables complete the scene.

The queen of repurposing, Marjorie crochets old plastic bags to create colourful hats, bags and coverings for disposable-but-useful containers.

The Story of our Romance

Our romance began at Campbell Town, Tas., towards the end of 1962, when common interests drew us together, and made us aware of each other. Although we were not free to marry, this awareness developed into mutual attraction. Many difficulties had to be overcome before we obtained freedom to marry. This freedom came on July 26th, 1966

C.E. Ball at City Hall Sept. 11th, 1964

A page from Marjorie's 1966 wedding scrapbook, commemorating her marriage to Adrian Cooper.

"I LOVE YOU" I DO I DO!

54

On a page of her 1976 wedding scrapbook, Marjorie is pictured with her third
husband, Eric Bligh. The bride wore a princess-line gown that she made from
blue embossed voile and white lace.

Eric models a tweedy green cardigan, hat and gloves set knitted by Marjorie.

Marjorie with her prize-winning table cover constructed from squares crocheted out of used pantyhose. Her hat and striped vest are knitted from the same.

Fingers busy as ever, Marjorie poses with her crocheting for the cover of the final edition of her signature household manual, At Home with Marjorie Bligh (1998).

In the mid-1990s Marjorie invited Ray Groom, then the Tasmanian premier, to Madden Street to see her books and taste her fare.

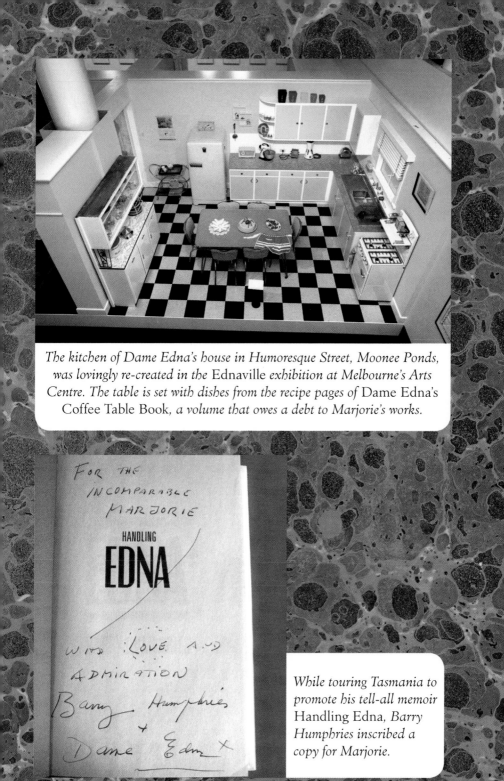

The kitchen of Dame Edna's house in Humoresque Street, Moonee Ponds, was lovingly re-created in the Ednaville exhibition at Melbourne's Arts Centre. The table is set with dishes from the recipe pages of Dame Edna's Coffee Table Book, a volume that owes a debt to Marjorie's works.

While touring Tasmania to promote his tell-all memoir Handling Edna, *Barry Humphries* inscribed a copy for Marjorie.

*On the replica Batman Bridge as it is today stand
94-year-old Marjorie and the writer Danielle Wood.*

Just married: Mr and Mrs Cooper begin their new life together.

visiting often and bringing flowers. But early one morning, when Marjorie rang Madden Street to have Adrian bring some items in to the hospital for her, he failed to answer the phone. Shortly after, a doctor came to Marjorie's bedside and gave her 'a pill' before breaking the news that Adrian had suffered a heart attack, and was now in the intensive care unit on the next floor of the same hospital. The news did nothing to speed Marjorie's recovery and she was kept in the hospital for several more miserable days, during which she was both very ill and frantic with worry, only able to make short, painful visits to Adrian's bedside.

If we read between the lines of the diaries, it seems that Marjorie had by now developed a mostly workable relationship with Adrian's daughters. His admission to hospital, however, redrew the battle lines. Adrian was only allowed a certain number of visitors at a time, and when some of Marjorie and Adrian's friends arrived Marjorie expected Adrian's children and their families to leave the room for a while. One of his daughters, however, believed that her claim to her father's bedside was greater, and so the friends went away without having seen the patient. Marjorie, fuming, retaliated by complaining to the nursing staff about her stepdaughter's 'performing', with the result that all visits to Adrian were limited to just a few minutes' duration.

While in hospital Adrian suffered a second heart attack; although he made enough of a recovery to be released into Marjorie's care, his health was now permanently fragile. One of Adrian's doctors recommended increased exercise after a period off work for recuperation, suggesting a daily walk of four miles. For a time Marjorie watched despairingly as Adrian walked the four miles each morning before starting work, often coming home too tired to eat dinner. Early 1971 saw Adrian relocated to a teaching position at a primary school much closer to home, but by now even the considerably shortened walk to school taxed his weakened body. Marjorie had refused to entertain the thought that Adrian was dying, but the notion must have been at the forefront of her mind in February 1971, when she learned that Cliff, aged 57, had 'dropped dead shearing sheep on his property'.

By June 1971 Adrian's health had deteriorated perilously. He was admitted to hospital suffering terrible pain, delirium and fever, and—despite doctors being upbeat about his prognosis—in low spirits.

TYPEWRITER KEYS DIRTY AND RIBBON HINT: Typewriter keys that become dirty and clogged up with dried ink can be cleaned with a piece of fresh putty about the size of a walnut. Press it on lightly. Knead it in your fingers and press it on again, and repeat until the keys are clean. Wipe keys with a piece of cotton wool dipped in lighter fluid or petrol to remove the thin film of oil left by the putty. When the ribbon loses all of its ink and starts printing lightly, remove it and put a few drops of oil on it. Roll it up and leave it for a while and it will renew itself.

Marjorie's diary entries from this period are marked by a particularly formulaic listing of details to do with her key topics: the weather, daily domestic activities, visits and correspondence, preparations for a forthcoming caravan holiday around Australia, concerns over Adrian's health.

Oyster (mock)

Cooked mashed brains, seasoned with salt and pepper and a little lemon juice. Mix into a rich, thick, white sauce and you'll have a mock filling for oyster patties.

Even the short entry for Wednesday, June 9 is relatively true to type: 'Did washing. Rained all morning. Went into Sims [neighbour] to put Adrian's pyjamas on her line in hot house. [Aunt] Ruby came in with hospital call to say Adrian passed away.'

A few days later a bewildered and distraught Marjorie buried the most beloved of her husbands. His headstone reads:

> Treasured and fond memories of Adrian H. C. Cooper, B.A. who departed this life June 9th, 1971, aged 58 years. Beloved husband of Marjorie, for five of our happiest years. Loved Pa of his children, step- and grandchildren.
> 'Underneath are the everlasting arms' Deut. 33 : 27.

We will never know how Marjorie's life might have turned out if she had not lost Adrian so early, for it was in the period of her deepest grief that she began to transform into the public figure that she has remained for the past four decades. Though she had written one book, and enjoyed the odd bit of celebrity that it brought her, it did not seem that she was burning with ambition to produce a second. But her friends, relatives and media contacts—having a sound understanding of her temperament—encouraged her to get on with writing projects that would absorb her energies, and alleviate her loneliness and boredom.

First, the 'social editress' of the *Advocate* visited Marjorie with a

(from) *Valentine's Day Recipes*

SWEETHEART SHAPE

1 large tin tomato juice (2 cups), 1 cup chopped tomatoes, 1 tablespoon vinegar, 1 teaspoon Worcestershire sauce, salt and pepper to taste, ½ lb. pork luncheon meat, 2 hard-boiled eggs, 1 oz. gelatine, 2 tablespoons stock or water, stuffed olives, salad greens to garnish.

Mix tomato juice and tomatoes together, add vinegar, sauce and seasonings. Chop meat into cubes and slice eggs. Soften gelatine in stock, place over hot water to dissolve. Dilute 1 teaspoon of this with another tablespoon of stock and pour over base of wetted (or slightly oiled) heart-shape mould. When beginning to set, arrange over the slices of egg. Allow to set, then fold in gelatine and meat into tomato juice. Spoon carefully over egg slices in mould. Chill, and when firm, turn onto serving dish. Garnish with salad, vegetables and olives.

PASSION FLUMMERY

Dissolve 2 tablespoons gelatine in 1 cup of water. Blend 2 tablespoons flour in another cup of water. Pour both mixtures into a saucepan, add ¾ cup sugar and bring to boil. Boil 5 minutes, stirring continuously. Add 1 cup passionfruit pulp and reheat to boiling. Cool and allow to partially set. Whisk until set and frothy.

TENDER KISSES

Cream 4 oz. each of butter and sugar with ½ teaspoon vanilla. Add an unbeaten egg. Work in 8 oz. plain flour that has been sifted twice with 3 teaspoons baking powder and pinch salt. Put into bag and pipe small rosettes on to a greased tray. Bake in a moderate oven 7 to 10 minutes. Allow to cool on trays. Join with jam or butter icing and dust with icing sugar.

LOVERS' KNOTS

Sift 6 oz. plain flour with ½ teaspoon baking powder. Rub in 4 oz. butter and 2 oz. sugar. Beat 1 small egg with a tablespoon cream and add to make a stiff dough. Leave in refrigerator 15 minutes. Cut into small pieces and roll into thin strips. Tie each strip into a knot, brush with milk and dip in crushed sugar. Bake 20 minutes in moderate oven.

proposal for a six-month trial column. Marjorie agreed, and on the second Saturday of January 1972 'Mrs Cooper's Tried 'n' True Hints' made its debut. Whizzing through the microfilm for the *Advocate* of that year, you can see names and phrases leap out: 'Nixon', 'Germaine Greer', 'Irish Peace', 'LSD'. Among these, in the 'Today's Woman' section, is Mrs Cooper, shown in a practical, no-nonsense headshot. For her first column she elected to feature an eggless batter for fish (eggs were 'still expensive', she noted), a hint about using pine detergent to combat aphids, advice about how to beat 'bulges' in the hems of flared skirts (now 'back in fashion') and a tip about cleaning your electric iron with toothpaste. Marjorie was an immediate success in her new role, and the column became a decades-long fixture in the *Advocate*.

Icing Substitute
Instead of icing a sponge, place paper d'oyley on top, then lightly sprinkle icing sugar over. Lift d'oyley off carefully.

As Marjorie was becoming increasingly well known through her column, Adrian's son Jim was urging his stepmother to consider producing a new edition of *Marjorie Blackwell at Home*. Accepting the challenge, Marjorie toiled throughout 1972 on the manuscript that would be published, in 1973, as *At Home with Marjorie Cooper*. In place of the spiral binding, sepia tones and fancy headings of her 1965 book, this updated edition featured glue binding, a cover in shades of orange and navy, and bold sans serif headings. In a tightly cropped cover shot, a more matronly Marjorie appears to be wearing a fur and drop earrings, her hair sternly disciplined into a smooth, curling coiffure.

'Dear Readers,' writes the 'authoress' in her preface. 'This is the second edition of my book—different title, because I remarried— with the majority of the contents the same, but with twice as many additions.' For the new edition Marjorie secured seven testimonial forewords, including one from the deputy prime minister, Lance

Barnard ('In the spirit of Mrs Beeton,' he wrote, 'this book details valuable information on how to eat with pleasure and prudence'), and placed them alongside ten of the eleven forewords from the first edition.

The new material reflects Marjorie's changed concerns and interests. Eight years on, she is more interested in beauty aids, weight control and looking after her health (as opposed to curing common ailments). A new section titled 'Around the World Recipes for Slimming' is dedicated to a series of fairly radical diets named after international locations (New York, Mexico, Spain, Italy, Switzerland, Canada, Norway, Argentina), each of which lays claim to swift and spectacular results. Another new section, 'Health Facts and Healthful Recipes', includes a run-down of the importance of major vitamins and minerals, and recipes incorporating such trendy new ingredients as millet meal, 'soya bean milk', lentils, lima beans and wheat germ. The legendary health of the Hunza people has also made it in: a description of their lifestyle sits alongside a selection of 'Hunza' recipes, including a drink based on coconut milk, which must have been relatively difficult to source in isolated mountainous pockets of northern Pakistan.

'Beauty from the Kitchen and Hints on Common Ailments', a

TWO EASY DIETS

THREE-DAY MILK AND BANANA DIET–
The average person will lose approximately 8 lbs. (3.6 kg) by setting aside
three days in which they just eat six ripe bananas and one pint (just over
½ a litre) of milk in a day.

ONE-DAY-A-WEEK ORANGE, MILK AND EGG DIET–
You should be able to shed 2 to 3 lbs (1–1½ kg) with ease, after a day of just
eating 4 oranges, 2 eggs and 2 pints (just over 1 litre) of milk. The eggs
must not be fried of course, but apart from that it doesn't matter how you
eat them. Scramble them in a little of the milk, boil, poach or coddle them.

third new section, betrays the influence of contemporary women's magazines. Here especially Marjorie abandons her usual writing style for a more colourful turn of phrase: 'Do you want hair that glistens with silky allure . . . skin that glows with the pale luminosity of a candle flame?' She quotes a 'Hollywood chemist and cosmetologist' who touts as hair treatments such common household items as apple cider vinegar, mayonnaise, skim milk, wheat germ oil, table salt, brewer's yeast, egg white and flat beer. She includes some treatments that are still in circulation ('make your eyes "sparkle" by placing cucumber rings on your eyelids'), and some that are not ('If you burn yourself, quickly pour treacle or golden syrup on to the burn. Relieves pain and leaves no scar').

The additions dilute Marjorie's emphasis on thrift and increase the scope of her cuisine. It seems that her expectations of material comfort have increased and her horizons have broadened, even if mostly through her reading material. Out are some of the offal recipes, and in are recipes based around such upmarket ingredients as crayfish, duck, goose and pheasant. While she keeps faith with her Tasmanian midlands origins and retains her recipes for mutton bird, hare, kangaroo and wattle bird, her soup section now includes a gazpacho and her dessert section a zabaglione.

The gardening section of *At Home with Marjorie Cooper* is also greatly expanded. Marjorie, in her foreword, puts this down to her 'added knowledge acquired the hard way, by trial and error'. She had become a 'pollution-conscious' gardener and signed up as treasurer of the new Devonport branch of the Organic Gardening Society (the founding of which she attributes to the now semi-retired ABC gardening guru Peter Cundall). Marjorie had also taken a trenchant position against the fluoridation of the water supply, and installed a rainwater tank in 1971 when the 'poisoning' began.

"Hangover" Cure

Half teaspoon Worcestershire sauce, pinch salt, squeeze lemon juice and one egg. Put all in glass (don't beat egg), close your eyes and down it in one gulp! or, use a mixture of ascorbic acid (Vitamin C) and fructose (apple juice). Lemons can be used for the same purpose without any added vitamin supplementation.

Bottles (medicine)

To catch drips and keep label clean, twist a pipe cleaner around neck of bottle.

Stockings or Pantyhose (care)

Double the life of your pantyhose or stockings by dissolving 1 level teaspoon gelatine in 1½ cups of hot water. Add cold water to make 6 cups. Squeeze pantyhose through this mixture several times, and hang over towel rail (do not wring). Wash in normal manner after each wearing, but re-dip after 7 wearings; or

Soak them when new for 24 hours in a tablespoon of salt and 3 cups of water; or

Wet new ones, wring out gently, place in a plastic bag and toss in the freezer. Once frozen, you thaw them out in the bath tub and then hang them up to dry.

Nerves on Edge

Add the juice of an orange to 2 tablespoons honey and beaten egg yolk, and a cup of low fat milk. Whip together. Drink first thing each morning. Very strengthening.

IN case of facial emergency simply follow these hints:

Get rid of that tired wishy-washy look with a brush of blusher.

Wrap a cube of ice in a handkerchief and massage it over those dark shadows under your eyes before applying concealing cream.

If your complexion is dull with clogged pores, simmer a handful of sage leaves in some rain water. Leave to cool, strain, then dab into the skin and leave to dry. Sage is miraculous.

Face Tension

Purse your lips and then let go, to relax tight lips that are caused by stress, and shows in the face.

Pantyhose Tips

If a ladder spoils one leg, cut it off, then wait till a ladder spoils a leg in another pair, and wear the two legs with a double top.

If your pantyhose sag or they will not quite come high enough, wet hands and run them up your legs and you'll be surprised how comfortable they will be.

Lingerie Tip

If your white nylon slip is "grey" and you want to revive it, make a pot of strong tea, and boil it in it, in an old saucepan for 5 minutes, and you have a delightful shade of biscuit. Good for lace articles too.

Hair (superfluous)

Bleach it with 3 drops of ammonia and 1 tablespoon of hydrogen peroxide (20 vol. strength). Leave on a minute. Make fresh each time.

Toothpaste Substitute

If you have strawberries, mash a couple and put on teeth and brush vigorously. It removes stains and yellowing.

Trouser Creases

Turn inside out and with a piece of dry soap, rub up and down the dent a few times. Turn to right side and press.

Hair Rollers

Put a shower cap on, before you put on, or take off, your clothes. Much easier.

Hair Greying

Toss 2 tablespoons dried sage together with two tablespoons each black tea and rum into three cups of boiling water. Cover. Simmer for 25 minutes. Then steep for several hours and strain. Rub a little of this liquid into the hair and scalp every day. When the right shade is reached, reduce the daily application; or,

Put one drop of castor oil on top of your head every night. It thickens hair also and makes it grow long and glossy. (Another of my mother's secrets); or,

Mix three tablespoons of instant coffee powder in a cup of boiling water. Allow to cool, add a little perfume, then pour over hair after washing. Or, put a teaspoon salt in 4 tablespoons brandy and rub on hair twice a week.

Ankles (thick):

Cross one leg over the other, and keeping your leg taut, draw circles in the air with your foot – 20 times each ankle.

Shoes (red)

If toes are badly scuffed, try red nail polish (of exact shade). Three or four coats are necessary.

REVIVING AN IRON:

Is your electric iron old and so hard to slide over the clothes? Give it a new lease of life by cleaning it with toothpaste, rubbing it hard with a cloth and rinsing all off with tepid water afterwards. You will be amazed at the dirt that comes off the iron on to the cloth.

Beach Towel Pocket

A small pocket on a beach towel is handy for holding keys, money, or a handkerchief, so turn over a corner, stitch one side and put a zip in the other.

Party Tip

Wipe light globes with French perfume for romantic occasions.

As well as containing masses of gardening information, practical tips and recipes for insecticides, the green-thumb section of Marjorie's second edition is concerned with the aesthetics of plants. She includes instructions for growing an apple in a bottle, drying decorative plants, creating bonsai plants and making ferns grow in interesting formations. She also lists five separate methods for 'skeletonising' leaves and flowers for display.

But perhaps the most noticeable difference between the first and second editions of Marjorie's household manual is the presence of Adrian Cooper. On the second page, a photograph of Marjorie and Adrian on their wedding day is surrounded by quotations and homilies on the subject of eternal love. Among the recipes are 'Adrian's Favourite Chocolate Cake', 'Adrian's Favourite Pavlova' and 'Adrian's Scones'. Into the new edition's final section, 'Poems I Love', Marjorie has given her love for Adrian and her grief over his death full coverage.

Camping Hints

Take your ironing board along with you when you next go caravanning. It comes in handy for an extra table for meals, writing, airing clothes, etc. Folds away for packing.

Keep flies at bay in the lavatory when out camping by putting ½ cup kerosene and 1 cup water into the tin first. The kerosene floats all the time until the tin is full, so forms a crust and prevents any odour. Also very good with people who have to use a commode.

Take some plastic garbage bags, and if it rains, you can soon convert them into a coverall for the children to hike around in.

She quotes 'a little verse I found in a pocket of one of my husband's coats after he passed away', as well as the lyrics of his favourite love songs, his favourite quotes and homilies. There is also a new selection of poems by Marjorie herself, mostly concerning her sorrow, but one thanking her friends for their support in her time of need.

Marjorie is not known for irony, so I suspect there was not even a twinkle of it in her eye when she selected the aphorism that would be the final item on the final page of *At Home with Marjorie Cooper*. It reads: 'If you want people to notice your faults, start giving advice.'

⌐▷●◁⌐

Grief, it is said, rewrites your address book. For Marjorie, Adrian's death brought new people into her life, such as the young Seventh Day Adventist pastor Michael Chamberlain, who visited and comforted her after she was widowed. Michael and his wife, Lindy, became firm friends of Marjorie's, and Marjorie became a regular at their church. In later years Marjorie was dumbfounded by the accusation that Lindy was guilty of murdering her baby, Azaria.

Adrian's death also served to restore Marjorie's relationship with her older sister, Doreen. The sisters had not been much in contact since the kerfuffle over Marjorie and Adrian's wedding, but when Adrian died Doreen immediately rang her sister and asked to come visit her. Marjorie was thereafter inclined to see Doreen's withdrawal from the bridal party as the fault of Doreen's husband, who had been friendly with Cliff.

Marjorie's relationships with her sisters seem to have been friable. Here and there in the diaries and autobiography are seemingly random comments about her and Beatrice 'burying the hatchet', or Beatrice being 'welcomed back into the fold', without the nature of the original conflict being disclosed. Marjorie and Doreen both loved their homes and gardens, and both were tireless workers, good seamstresses and cooks. But they had their points of divergence, too. As Marjorie recounts:

> She was thorough in all she did, but was very, very frank, and very wasteful. I've been staying with her when she has announced, 'It's handbag day, today,' and into the incinerator would go a heap of

handbags to burn. She periodically had 'shoe' days, 'clothes' days and 'other' days too, because she tired of things so quickly.

Doreen and Marjorie's reconciliation in 1971 was timely, as Doreen had not much longer to live. She died in 1973 from cancer, and Marjorie was among those to care for her at the end.

Marjorie was intent on keeping up relations with her stepdaughters, and contacted one of them to say that she was going to come by with Christmas presents for her family. The 'reply was that I was not to call with presents at Christmas, or any other time,' she writes. Other relationships also took a knock. The pampered poodle Freda Fi Fi found life different after Adrian's death, and became destructive. After she chewed up a rug and damaged the laundry door Freda had her indoor and porch privileges withdrawn, but even when she was shut in the garage she managed to get into mischief, ripping open garbage bags and strewing the contents. It seems that, in Adrian's absence, she attached herself not to Marjorie but to Adrian's son Jim and his family, who often babysat her when Marjorie went away.

(from a foreword to *At Home with Marjorie Cooper*)

Couple together boundless energy, tremendous enthusiasm for life and insatiable love of home, garden, friends and creative activity and you almost have Marj Cooper. A friendly approach, engaging personality, whose mind ranges over a multitude of topics and who derives joy and happiness from involvement in community life in its many forms but yet whose heart is in home and family and you have this warm, friendly and down to earth personality. Marj Cooper has packed into her busy life much more than most people achieve in a life time, yet she is still to be found adding to the beauty of her environment, tending her garden, busy with her handicrafts and contributing to the media on a range of subjects of local interest.

DON DEVITT,
Senator for Tasmania

Any time the Cooper family visited me I had trouble with Freda Fi Fi after they went home. She sulked, wouldn't eat for days and cried at night, because they nursed her and made a fuss of her. She even climbed into their car, and when I would try to get her out, she would bare her teeth at me.

At Home with Marjorie Cooper was launched in the backyard at Madden Street on November 24, 1973. Or, to be accurate, the cover of the book was launched that day. To Marjorie's intense frustration, there were no actual copies of the book available for the launch because the company she had engaged to do the printing and binding had failed to complete the job. Over the weeks that followed the company fed copies through to Marjorie in dribs and drabs, but there were missing, crookedly cut and uncut pages that made them unfit to sell. It was an expensive headache for Marjorie, and many surviving copies show evidence of poor production. My copy—inherited from my grandmother—is more or less unbound, having degenerated into a collection of loose leaves.

Despite the humiliation of having only a cover, and the disappointment of losing a hundred-plus sales to those present at the gathering, Marjorie managed to enjoy herself at the launch of *At Home with Marjorie Cooper*. She had cooked up a storm, and a trestle table in the garden was laid out with all manner of goodies, each offering labelled so that her guests could later refer to the relevant recipes from her book. A Tasmanian senator, Don Devitt, gave the launch speech ('ON ME,' shrieks a joyful Marjorie in her diary entry for the day), while Devonport's Congregational Church minister blessed the cover (and the next day, in church, 'even mentioned my achievements in his address from the pulpit'). Also present at the

Freda Fi Fi, seen here with a selection of toys knitted by Marjorie, was like a child for the Coopers.

launch was somebody who would feature large in Marjorie's life for the next two years: a new dancing partner, adversary, flame. In her autobiography she dubs him 'Buoy'.

Buoy's strong points seem to have been that he was debonair, danced well, liked to give and receive gifts, and had a strong command of social charm. But his behaviour at the launch ought to have sounded a warning bell to Marjorie. Far from being a model of supportiveness, he sloped off during the speeches, without even saying goodbye to the lady of the moment. Later, he would explain that he had left after overhearing someone gossiping that he was only going out with Marjorie for her money. Based on Marjorie's accounts of his subsequent behaviour, though, it's possible to infer that the reason he left the launch was because the limelight wasn't big enough for the two of them.

From the beginning, Marjorie's 'unbalanced friendship' with Buoy was a wild ride. No sooner had the attraction sparked than Buoy rang Marjorie to tell her that he didn't want to see her anymore, 'because he didn't like Scrabble and I was always too busy when he called'. Wounded and dismayed, Marjorie phoned him back later the same day and the pair reconnected, but she noted in her

(from) HINTS FOR HORS D'OEUVRES, DRINKS AND SAVOURIES Etc.

Cut some white or brown bread into finger lengths. Fry each in hot oil after being dipped quickly in cold milk. Drain on brown paper. Spread with mayonnaise and top with a sardine.

Frosted grapes make an attractive party dish. Wash and dry well, then dip in whipped egg-white, toss in castor sugar, and dry on a rack.

Imitation carrots look very realistic and a friend (the late Mrs. Knowles) gave me this recipe: – Take 1 teaspoon butter and 1 teaspoon Kraft cheese. Colour with cochineal. Shape in to a miniature carrot and put a tiny sprig of parsley in the crown. Place each one on a buttered savoury biscuit.

If you want coloured eggs for your savoury eggs or salad, boil them in the water that you have left over from your redbeet. What a colourful salad you will have.

Grill a piece of bacon that has been wrapped around a prune or ripe banana and held by a tooth-pick.

Another suggestion for the party table: Take oranges and cover with tooth-picks. Make some cream cheese, mix with chopped parsley into a paste. Form into balls and push one on each tooth-pick. Soak some prunes in gin or sherry, then make a jelly with the gin or sherry and half water and gelatine. Dip the prunes that have been on a tooth-pick into the jelly and when almost set, take out and stick into an orange.

Cut Belgium sausage into slices (thinly). Insert a small coloured onion in centre of each slice and roll up. Push a small coloured onion onto a tooth-pick, then through the roll of sausage, then finish with another differently coloured onion. Place on plate.

Cut a pineapple in half lengthwise and scoop out pineapple and cut into squares. Put back in pineapple case and top with cream.

diary that if it happened again she wouldn't be the one doing the 'crawling'. According to Marjorie, Buoy would be gentlemanly at social gatherings until the conversation focused on Marjorie, and then he would sulk. He expected her to drop everything when he came to visit, and to sit and listen to his long monologues. 'His idea of an ideal partner was a mute one,' Marjorie writes.

If there weren't already sufficient bad omens of trouble on the horizon, there were also the events of the holiday on Flinders Island that Marjorie and Buoy took together at the beginning of 1974. There, they stayed with friends of Buoy's, a married couple, and Marjorie was much miffed by the flirtatious antics between Buoy and the wife. In her diary she records how Buoy and his friend repeatedly used a 'four letter word starting with c', presumably in more than Scrabble, and it's not difficult to imagine Marjorie becoming increasingly prim and huffy. During the Flinders Island trip Marjorie was also urging Buoy to give up a 'dirty little habit', which—judging by some newspaper clippings pasted into her 1974 diary—seems to have referred to his cigarette smoking.

The cornerstone of their relationship was attending dances together, but even these events rarely went smoothly. Buoy didn't like Marjorie to watch him when he danced with other partners, or to cramp his style by sitting too close to him when resting between dances. For her part, Marjorie disliked that Buoy would come to visit in the evenings and leave at about 8.30. Rather than starting a new project at that time, Marjorie would go to bed—'wasting precious hours'.

PRESS-STUDS

Press-stud pairs should always be
Matched with perfect symmetry.

Sew the knobs with even spacing
Neatly to the upper facing.

Then, with tailor's chalk applied,
Press them to the underside.

Chalk marks now will clearly show
Where the matching half should go.

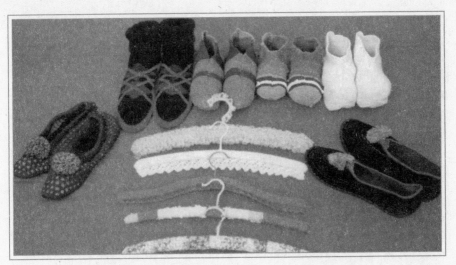

A small selection of craft items created by the ever-productive Marjorie.

To me 1974 was a year wasted in my life. I don't think I slept soundly any one night, and I never knew each morning, what would happen before night fall as far as being happy, or sad was concerned. Because I was desperately lonely I kept the friendship with 'Buoy' going, but I should have shown him the door, because he had a split personality. He could change in a second from an angel to a devil.

And yet the relationship continued. Marjorie and Buoy saw each other most days, except when he was having a 'fit of the no-speaks', and the pair did a remarkable amount for each other. When Buoy moved into a new flat Marjorie took on the project of whipping his garden into shape, and when he had a heart attack and spent a few weeks in hospital Marjorie used the opportunity to replace the carpet in his flat, polish the floors and clean the place from top to bottom. By the time he was released from hospital his place 'was looking like a home, not a house'. The assistance was not one-sided. Buoy frequently used his handyman skills to make useful changes to the fixtures at Mar-ian.

HINTS FOR SCONES

Melt butter before adding to flour; if used solid, it can show up as patches in finished scones. Knead dough very lightly with hand – only until smooth. Pat out scones lightly by hand, then roll lightly to required thickness. Do not roll right to edge; this rolls out air. Roll only to smooth mixture, then round edges with hand. Scone tray should be lightly greased only – never floured. After cooking, cover scones with clean cloth to keep soft.

Add a teaspoon of cornflour to the flour when you are making scones and note the difference, a lighter scone.

Put stale scones in a covered saucepan over a low heat for 5 minutes or more – results in fresher scones and less electricity than heating in the oven. If you want to freshen a stale scone or two IN the oven, first dip quickly in milk, wrap in foil and heat through in oven. Bread can be treated the same. Like fresh scones.

ADRIAN'S SCONES

1 egg, 1 dessertspoon sugar, 1 tablespoon melted butter, ¾ cup milk, 2 cups S.R. flour, ½ teaspoon salt, milk for glazing.
Beat egg and sugar together until thick; add melted butter to milk. Sift together flour and salt into mixing bowl; make a well in centre. Stir in egg mixture, then milk, mix to a soft dough. Turn out on to floured board, knead lightly. Pat or roll out to ½ in. thickness, cut out with floured scone-cutter. Place on lightly greased scone slide, brush tops with a little cold milk. Bake in hot oven 10–12 minutes. Makes 1 dozen.

MARJORIE'S SCONES

You can have these in the oven 5 minutes after you start preparing them, they are so easy to make.

Sift 2 cups S.R. flour with a teaspoon of salt into a basin. Make a well in the centre and tip in one-third cup of peanut oil that has been mixed with two-thirds cup of milk. Mix with a fork and then knead into shape, using no more flour. Cut into rounds and put on greased paper and cook for 10 minutes in a hot oven.

ADRIAN'S FAVOURITE PAVLOVA

Beat the whites of 4 eggs with a pinch of salt for 6 mins., gradually adding 8 oz. castor sugar, 1 teaspoon vinegar and ½ teaspoon vanilla essence. Beat until stiff. Sift in 1 level dessertspoon of cornflour and blend in lightly. Pre-heat oven to 400 deg. Put Pavlova in, on prepared tray, turn oven down to 250 deg.

and bake undisturbed for 1¼ hours. No longer. Rises high when cooking, but falls towards end of cooking time.

ADRIAN'S FAVOURITE CHOCOLATE CAKE (quick-mix)

1 cup S.R. flour (or one cup plain flour and 1 teaspoon baking powder, which incidentally makes the nicer cake), 2 eggs, 1 cup sugar, ½ teaspoon vanilla, 2 tablespoons cocoa, 2 oz. butter, ½ cup milk.

Put all dry ingredients into mixing bowl. Melt butter and add to milk, then beat on mixer for 3 to 5 minutes. Put into a well-greased tin and bake in mod. oven (300 deg.) for ¾ of an hour.

Love Cake No. 1

Mix together 1 shady tree, 1 small seat, 4 lips (well pressed), 2 hands (well clasped), and allow to remain 2 hours after dark. Sufficient for 2 persons only.

Love Cake No. 2

Mix 4 oz. kisses, 4 sweet lips (pressed well together with 2 oz. love) and ½ oz. each of teasing and squeezing. Bake well together in a young man's arms, and serve in the dark.

Sponge Cake (blow away, Adrian's favourite)

Beat for 5 minutes, 3 eggs and ½ cup sugar. Add 1 teaspoon golden syrup and beat another 10 minutes. Sift 3 times the following: 1 tablespoon flour, ½ cup arrowroot, 1 teaspoon cream of tartar, ½ teaspoon bicarb. soda, 2 teaspoons ginger, 1 teaspoon cocoa and ½ teaspoon cinnamon. Fold into egg mixture and pour into 2 greased sandwich tins and bake in moderate oven for 10 minutes. When cold, ice with a butter icing with ½ teaspoon spice added to it, and walnuts placed on top to decorate. Fill with sweetened whipped cream, flavoured with spice.

In addition to the practical generosity, Marjorie and Buoy also lavished expensive gifts upon each other. It's unlikely that all this giving was straightforward in its intent, for as the relationship became increasingly toxic it was gifts that both parties used as their weapons of choice. After a row in early 1975 Marjorie began to be besieged by boxes of produce—first cherry plums, then vegetables—left on her Madden Street doorstep. 'After box after box of vegetables had greeted me on the front door step in January,' she writes, 'I retaliated by taking a hamper to his flat after dark, but mine contained patties, cakes, scones, pudding, meringue and a roast of beef.'

Throughout 1975 the stress of this complicated relationship took its toll. Marjorie entered fewer shows and temporarily lost contact with some of her friends. But still she kept herself busy. She decided to refresh her driving skills, and after seven lessons she 'had enough confidence' to buy herself a gold automatic Escort. Given her accounts of her early experiences on the road, it's questionable that

PIZZA PIE

Make favourite scone dough. Roll out very thin. Place on pizza pan and firmly press edge of dough on to edge of pan. Sprinkle with ½ cup grated Mozzarella cheese. Then cover with Pizza Sauce and more grated cheese. Bake 425 deg. for 15–20 minutes (until crust is brown and cheese melted).

PIZZA SAUCE: Saute ¼ cup coarsely chopped onion in ½ oz. (1 tablespoon) salad or olive oil in saucepan, add 1 large can whole tomatoes (mash the tomatoes), 1 can tomato paste, 1 bay leaf, 1 teaspoon salt, 1 teaspoon sugar, a dash of pepper, 1 clove garlic, 1 teaspoon dried oregano leaves (or ½ teaspoon crushed oregano). Bring to boiling over medium heat. Simmer, stirring occasionally until thick. Variations: Any of the following may be added: mushrooms, ¼ lb. Italian sausage (cut up), green pepper, olives, cheddar cheese, anchovy, sardines.

MY LETTER TO THE ONE I LOVED

No letter that I write to you
Says half the things I mean it to!

For how can words reveal a part
Of all the longing in my heart?

No pen and ink can translate this –
The tender sweetness of a kiss –

Nor any word convey as much
As just a smile – a look – a touch . . .

How weak are words that can but say:
I love and miss you more each day!

this confidence was well founded. 'Sometimes going out my drive,' she writes, 'I'd pull on the wheel the wrong way, so I just went the way the car wanted to go, and turned down another street.'

Marjorie was also making improvements at Mar-ian. She came up with the idea of installing a scale replica of the Batman Bridge in the backyard. The full-size bridge had been built across the Tamar River in the late 1960s and, other than being the first cable-stayed bridge constructed in Australia, it doesn't have any particular claim to fame, or beauty. However, Marjorie toiled away alongside Buoy in order to create her vision of a backyard masterpiece. A long cement pool, filled with water, represents the Tamar River over which the miniature bridge spans. Marjorie added miniature picnic tables beside the bridge, planted out dwarf conifers and put fish in the pond. As Climar had once been in Campbell Town, Mar-ian was

MISSED

Missed in the mornings when the day brings once more
The sound of my animals outside the door;
The breakfast to cook and the kitchen to clean.
The old happy round of the daily routine.
Missed when the kettle is boiling for tea –
Setting the tray when it's only for me!
Why bake a cake when there's no one to share?
Tea on your own is a lonely affair.
Missed in the evenings when fires die away,
Missed at the end of another long day . . .
Missed in a hundred and one little things.
In every corner, and outside too, a memory clings.
                                    Oh, how I miss you.

now an attraction of sorts, and school children came on excursions
to see the bridge that Marjorie built.

In early 1976 Marjorie and Buoy's relationship came to a rather
unusual end. By now, Marjorie suspected that she was not the only
woman in Buoy's life, and she would later come to believe that she
had been two-timed for the duration of their attachment. It was not
infidelity that was the last straw, however, but nudity. Arriving at
Madden Street in a state of excitement, Buoy invited Marjorie over
to his house saying that he had something to show her. She duly
accompanied him back to his flat in his car.

Marjorie tends to the plants in her porch at Mar-ian, Madden Street, Devonport. The name is a combination of the first three letters of her name and the last three of Adrian's.

IN YOUR COMPANY

Why is your Friendship such a dear and precious thing to me?
I think it is because when I am in your company
My better self comes uppermost in all I say and do.
Through your eyes I see things from a higher point of view.
My weaknesses you overlook, my failings you ignore;
You draw what is best in me and bring it to the fore.
In the radiance of your mind a different world I see;
I'm something more than just myself when in your company.

My Darling Adrian

I have never been more disgusted in my life, when, on entering that kitchen, I saw, hanging on the wall above the refrigerator, a huge picture of a nude woman in a disgraceful pose. *'Nakedness is uncomely in the mind as well as in body.'* He was grinning like a Cheshire cat, but I was very annoyed and embarrassed, so refused to sit in the room.

Marjorie's reaction sent Buoy into a rage and he ordered Marjorie out of his house. She believes that he deliberately shocked her into ending their friendship, rather than disclosing that he was in love with someone else. Whether Marjorie's theory is correct, or whether Buoy was just excited to show Marjorie a work of art that he loved, we will never know. But in the days that followed Buoy returned Marjorie's photographs and wrote her a letter of farewell. The two went their separate ways—though Marjorie has retained a list of those items he failed to return: new hedge clippers, six glass cloches, a fish tank, a washing machine cord and an embroidered hanky that had belonged to Adrian.

The split left Marjorie relieved but lonely. However, it would be only a few months before she would find the ideal companion for the next chapter of her life.

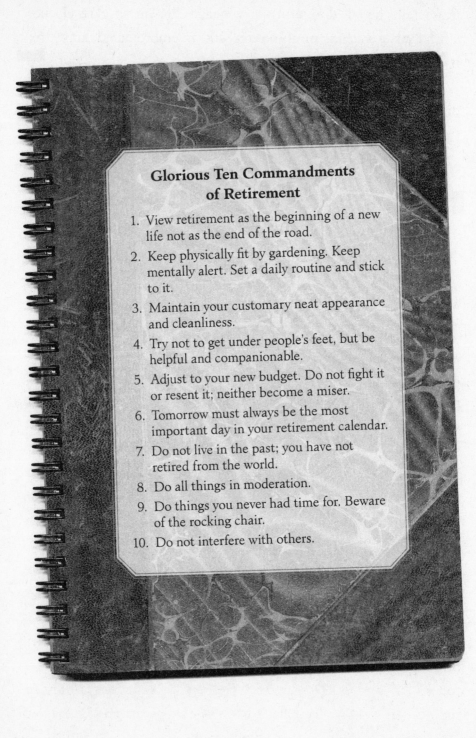

Glorious Ten Commandments of Retirement

1. View retirement as the beginning of a new life not as the end of the road.

2. Keep physically fit by gardening. Keep mentally alert. Set a daily routine and stick to it.

3. Maintain your customary neat appearance and cleanliness.

4. Try not to get under people's feet, but be helpful and companionable.

5. Adjust to your new budget. Do not fight it or resent it; neither become a miser.

6. Tomorrow must always be the most important day in your retirement calendar.

7. Do not live in the past; you have not retired from the world.

8. Do all things in moderation.

9. Do things you never had time for. Beware of the rocking chair.

10. Do not interfere with others.

4

Marjorie Bligh

I N her years as Mrs Blackwell and Mrs Cooper, Marjorie occupied a cosy niche in the hearts and kitchens of Tasmania, but it was as Mrs Bligh that she would achieve her peak of local fame and notoriety. Today, on the recipe shelves of many Tasmanians, you are likely to find one of Marjorie's spiral-bound and individually signed household manuals cosying up to the Jamie Olivers and Nigella Lawsons, Stephanie Alexanders and Matthew Evanses. In several kitchens I have visited Marjorie's tomes sit—physically, and in esteem—alongside the trusted intergenerational Tasmanian home-economics text *The Central Cookery Book*.

It was as Mrs Bligh that Marjorie published five of her six books, including her monumentally detailed 1986 autobiography, *Life Is for Living: The Heartaches and Happiness of Marjorie Bligh: With Snippets of Travel, Wisdom and History*. From Marjorie's stockpile in Madden Street books were dispatched to destinations around the country—to all states and territories except the Northern Territory, Marjorie reports—as well as across the globe. When Charles and Diana tied the knot, in 1981, Marjorie popped one of her books in the post as a wedding present; she also sent copies of her books to Ronald and Nancy Reagan at the White House and, more recently, to The Lodge for the edification of the then prime minister, Kevin Rudd.

In the Bligh years Marjorie expanded her repertoire, publishing not only on home economics but also on gardening, history and craft. As times changed, and Marjorie adjusted to life in an increasingly throwaway society, her thrifty ways attained new dimensions. She became locally famous for her crusade against useful resources being poured into landfill. Her response to the perceived crisis was to get busy with needles and hooks, knitting and crocheting disposable goods into new, reusable items. Say the name Marjorie Bligh, and many Tasmanians' thoughts will leap to the cunning repurposing of discarded plastic bags and pantyhose.

It was also as Mrs Bligh that Marjorie became more widely recognised as a personality, not only a homemaker and dispenser of household advice. Journalists, realising that Marjorie was always good for a bold statement and a quirky quip, began to fill newspaper pages and television screens with her wit and wisdom. Marjorie was put forward as both the symbol and chief proponent of lost domestic arts, her advancing years dovetailing neatly with a growing nostalgia for the apparent simplicity of yesteryear.

The Bligh years began in 1976, with Marjorie's high-speed marriage to the smiling, silver-haired bus driver Eric Bligh. On July 7 of that year Marjorie went by bus with a group of Devonport women to a CWA exhibition in Hobart. In her diary entry for the day she records no significant information other than that the bus was driven by a

Eric Bligh, the bus driver who became Marjorie's third husband.

'Mr Blythe', and that she had been feeling depressed after reading love letters written by her 'darling' (presumably Adrian). But when she tells the story of this day in *Our Wedding Book*, a cream-covered purpose-made scrapbook identical to the one in which she commemorated her second marriage, she records the events in more detail. Under the heading 'The Story of Our Romance', she writes:

Prior to our meeting on July 31st, my step-son (Bruce Cooper) told me about a colleague who he was anxious for me to meet, because he had previously lost a wife & was very lonely. He praised his virtues highly, and likewise Bruce told Eric the same things about me, as I was available too. Nothing eventuated from that, but on the 7th July Eric drove 22 C.W.A. ladies to an exhibition in Hobart. I sat up the front with my friend Francy Salter & she reminded me that the driver had lost his wife and that he would be a good mate for me. It was not until the return trip home, that I could pluck up the courage to tell him who I was. It happened like this. I said to Eric 'Do you know Bruce Cooper?' He replied 'I'll say I do.' Then I said '<u>Well</u>, I'm his stepmother.' To me, Eric didn't seem interested, but I noticed he adjusted the mirror a little. I thought it was to watch the passengers up the back, but now I know it was to study me more closely. I had bought some fruit cake at the exhibition, and invited Eric for supper, but on arrival at Devonport, I chickened out.

Despite all that passed between Marjorie and Eric on July 7, Marjorie counts July 31 as the official date of their meeting. This was the day that the phone rang at Madden Street and an unidentified caller asked, 'Have you got any of that fruit cake left?' Once Marjorie had twigged that it was the bus driver, she invited him over to her place that very night.

In their short courtship Eric impressed Marjorie by taking her to his 'spotless' house and showing her his bottle collection. (Eric's treasures were so remarkable, apparently, that Marjorie took a steady

AS I write this . . . I still have jet lag, and for those who don't know what that means, you tend to walk sideways and bump into everything. You cannot concentrate; in fact the feeling is similar to being awakened suddenly out of a deep sleep [and stumbling] out of bed to answer the phone as if half unconscious. Other than that, my stomach is back to normal and I am eating. I miss my own food when I am away. We eat onions every day at home but they are seldom in your food when away, only a trace or two in England in bread rolls. I am so happy to be home and Eric and I have been right round the world now, and I have to confess, no place matches Tasmania. You can eat anything without fear of diarrhoea and the water is clean and one blessing is that when you arrive at our airport you don't have to show passports, queue, or open your luggage.

Holidays are wonderful if you have time off for relaxing at each place, harmony, adequate sleep, have food you like, and if you don't have to wait around at airports. I just detest that; also queuing, showing passports, filling out forms, travelling long hours without a break, irregular meals and not enough cooked vegetables, smoke drifting onto you from smokers, mineral water, aching legs, and "stinking" face washers.

stream of her friends and relatives to Eric's home to inspect them.) Eric told Marjorie that since his wife had died, five months earlier, he had been sitting at home in the evenings drinking, smoking, watching television, and eating fish and chips. No doubt Marjorie knew

Hat (travelling)
Put the crown inside an empty ice-cream container, and pack clothes under the hat brim.

that she could put all of this to rights in a jiffy. And indeed, Eric gave up smoking on the spot. By August 2 Marjorie declared their attraction to be 'love at first sight', by August 9 Eric had proposed marriage, and by August 14 the engagement notice was in the local press and the wedding date set for September 18.

It can be difficult to keep pace with Marjorie's gender politics, yet the circumstances of her third marriage provide insight. As a career housewife Marjorie found herself challenged in the wake of Adrian's death to work out how to wife a house that had no husband in it. Without someone whose deficiencies required the counterbalance of her competencies she felt all at sea. Buoy's intermittent affections had kept her somewhat romantically occupied, but there was still nobody in the house who provided a focus for Marjorie's daily whirl of domestic activity.

While Marjorie tells us that women ought not nag their husbands to do the washing up ('that's *your* job'), and while the thought of a woman at the controls of an aeroplane is enough to make her hyperventilate ('I went cold all over and had to sit down or I would have fallen over,' she writes of her discovery that a domestic flight she was boarding would be piloted and co-piloted by women: 'I felt suddenly ill, and thought I was choking, as I told them I could not possibly go any further with women at the controls'), she has in recent years been pleased to see women step into the roles of Australia's governor-general and prime minister. As women are better than men at running a house, she says, it stands to reason that they would also be better at running a country. From Marjorie's writings, it would appear that her expectations of how women and men ought to behave are as pink and blue as you can get. But in none of her three marriages did she enact the passive, subservient, dependent wifely role that she seems to extol. Yes, she served her husbands by cooking, shopping, cleaning, washing and ironing, but she always earned money that she considered hers and had control of how that money was spent. Moreover, she was the key decision maker in all the households of which she was mistress. Marjorie loves the male of the species, and has enormous respect for men who hold public positions she regards as particularly

(from) Holiday Hints

A useful hold-all when travelling is a cushion cover – you can put your night clothes in it, and use it as a cushion during the day.

Place a thin layer of foam rubber on the bottom of the soap container to absorb moisture and you won't have a messy container. Carry a tube of shaving cream. Only a small squeeze is needed to wash hands.

Before packing, make a list of your requirements in duplicate. Stick one copy inside the lid of the suitcase for return journey packing. Tick off items as you pack.

Remember to smear petroleum jelly on your bath and basin before leaving so drops won't leave a brown mark.

When travelling on long distances, take a small well-filled foam rubber cushion and rest your feet on it. You won't feel the vibration so much, so legs won't be aching at the end of the journey.

Jet Lag

. . . I read once that if you put your feet into brown paper bags, crumbled up a bit first, then pull on your stockings and push your feet into old slippers for the long journey, it is a sure cure for jet lag. It helps the circulation, earths you and keeps your feet warm.

Holiday Packing: When packing for a trip where a lot of shopping is planned, take two suitcases. Fill a small case with your clothes and pack it inside a larger one which can be used for bringing your purchases home. Paint corners of suitcase a bright colour and they'll be easily identified at the airport.

important (medical, legal, religious), but privately she regards men as a bit hopeless on the home front. I suspect that when she leapt at the chance to make Eric her husband, she wasn't so much in need of a man to provide for her as a man she could care for.

Still, it was important to Marjorie that her third marriage be a proper romance, complete with a sense of destiny, love at first sight and the prospect of living happily ever after. On Marjorie and Eric's closer inspection, there turned out to be many coincidences that provided retrospective proof that their love was always meant to be. Eric had been Marjorie's favourite bus driver in Devonport in the early 1970s, the one who always helped her onto the bus with her groceries. And, back in the 1940s, Eric (then a soldier) had once asked a pretty girl to join him on the floor at a dance in Ross. She replied, 'I can't as my husband is a vicious man, and he'd kill you and me too.' Marjorie writes in the 1976 iteration of *Our Wedding Book*: 'and he's been in love with <u>that</u> girl ever since.'

Stockings (old) Put to Good Use

Cut spirally, making one long piece when finished and use it for knitting slippers, shopping bags, bath mats, etc.

The pair melded their lives at breakneck speed. By August 29 Eric had changed his will and invited real estate agents to look over his family home, so that he could put it on the market and move in with Marjorie. But in all the excitement Marjorie forgot to take note of some of her own advice. *First, find out if he has daughters*, she might have whispered to herself. For Eric, like Adrian, was the father of three girls.

———◆———

There were many similarities between the circumstances of Marjorie's third marriage and those of her second. Once again, Marjorie spent the period in the lead-up to the wedding suffering from illness and stress. Nevertheless, she spent hours hard at work at the sewing machine, making for herself a princess-line gown in embossed blue voile with a centre panel of white lace. She also made a flared blue jersey frock for her matron of honour, Beatrice, and a white suit for one of Adrian's grandsons, who would take the role of pageboy. And, once again, there was a bridesmaid dilemma. The plan had been for one of Eric's daughters to be a secondary attendant, alongside Beatrice, but just before the wedding the young woman pulled out, 'for reasons unknown'. For a second time Marjorie found herself bewildered that the children of her fiancé were not taking her into their hearts with alacrity; perhaps she underestimated the difficulty of burying a mother, watching a family home go on the market and accepting a new stepmother, all in the space of six months.

Marjorie was so ill with a 'nervous stomach' that she was unable to attend the rehearsal for her wedding. There was even talk that she might have to sit in a chair at the altar during the event. But when the

> The Canberra International Hotel has a dining room with a unique canopied garden atrium with sparkling rock pools among the Cocos Island Palms to have a chat beneath. It is one of the best my husband and I have stayed in in the world.
>
> C ome ye, who love her dark encircling hills,
> A cclaim the spreading beauty of the scene
> N ature devised – and Man's progressive art,
> B estowed in ordered plan and gardens fair.
> E xtol this symbol of our nationhood,
> R eserved to form Australia's glowing heart.
> R esponsive ever to a people's pride –
> A shrine – an inspiration to us all.

wedding day dawned, on September 18, it was 'only determination' that got her out of bed, into her gown and down to Devonport's Congregational Church on the arm of her son Ross. At the door she was met by what she describes as 'an ugly scene', created by 'a person protesting against Eric's re-marrying'. From Marjorie's diary it appears that the 'scene' might

> **False Teeth Safe**
> Half fill your handbasin with water before you clean your false teeth, then if you happen to drop them, the water breaks the fall. Over the years I have chipped pieces of my teeth through dropping them into the empty basin, but not since I've tried this.

have been another of Eric's daughters saying something snippy as Marjorie began her walk up the aisle. Yet in every other way the wedding—performed by the minister who married Marjorie and Adrian, ten years earlier—was a spectacular success. In her diary Marjorie records both her satisfaction with the event and her disappointment over her stepdaughter's 'disgraceful' behaviour, along with a note to herself: 'It will keep.'

If ever Marjorie's relatives and friends had the sense that she was keeping careful account of interpersonal credits and debits, it's possibly because she was. In the months following her wedding to Eric, Marjorie began to experience particular difficulties with one of Eric's daughters—not the one who bunked out of bridesmaid duty, nor the one who was out of sorts at the wedding, but the one she had initially found most simpatico. Marjorie kept careful note in her diaries of all the transactions between herself and this stepdaughter. Over the course of several months she records all the items given ('free') in the wash-up of Eric selling the family home: phone calls made

> **NOT ENOUGH WOOL?:** If you are in doubt about not having enough wool to finish a sweater, knit the sleeves and back first, then put contrasting bands or Fair Isle on the front.

and received, visits and gifts exchanged, a sum of money loaned, and one terrible insult received. This last item referred to the stepdaughter having sold a copy of *At Home with Marjorie Cooper* that had been given as a gift.

First-hand evidence of what Cliff, Adrian and Eric thought about life with Marjorie is thin on the ground. But in the 1976 *Our Wedding Book* is a glimpse of Eric's perspective on his first year as Marjorie's husband. Pasted into the final pages are the greeting cards that Marjorie and Eric exchanged on their first wedding anniversary. Eric's reads:

> To My Darling Marjorie
> On our first Wedding Anniversary, I want to thank you for all the love and presents & everything else you have given & done for me over the past year. We have had quite a bit of unhappiness, on account of the way my girls have treated us & their attitude towards you, but that has not altered my <u>love</u> for you one scrap & nothing ever will. There have been others who have tried to interfere, but with no success, only to make our love stronger for each other, so Darling thank you for everything & may we share many more anniversaries. I love you Darling. More every Day.
>
> Your loving husband Eric

The weeks before and months after the wedding were turbulent for Marjorie, Eric and their children, but in the years that have passed at least some of the bonds have repaired and strengthened. Today, among the key people upon whom Marjorie relies are a stepdaughter and stepson-in-law gained through her marriage to Eric.

≈※≈

In November 1976 the *Advocate* caught up with the times and changed the title of Marjorie's hint column to reflect her new name.

Marjorie, Freda Fi Fi and Eric at Madden Street, soon after their wedding.

'Mrs Bligh's Tried 'n' True Hints' debuted with a suggestion for making appealing children's cushions out of novelty hankies, a tip on making casseroles and stews taste better through the addition of a generous tablespoon of cream, and some suggestions for alternatives to using (hard-to-get) saltpetre when corning beef. There were also some words from the columnist, who told her readers that although she had remarried she looked forward to 'maintaining the quantity and quality' of her weekly hints. But Marjorie would do more than maintain her publishing output. Following her marriage to Eric she embarked on a new phase of productivity.

In 1981 Marjorie compiled and augmented her column hints,

and published *Marjorie Bligh's Homely Hints on Everything*, which contained about 3,500 hints and sold more than a thousand copies in the first two weeks after its release. She followed the success of the hint book in 1982 with her first green-thumb manual, *A–Z of Gardening*, and a third edition of her original household manual, this time with the title *At Home with Marjorie Bligh*. The gardening book takes its readers from Abelia to Zygocactus via a wealth of home-grown advice on growing indoor plants, flowers, trees, herbs and vegetables. The approach is largely organic, with Marjorie foreswearing commercially produced chemicals in favour of more wholesome pest remedies. Dedicated to Eric, her helpmeet in the garden, the book is also scattered with poetry and homilies.

The third edition of the staple household manual is evidence of Marjorie's attempts to swim with the tide of progress. Not only does this edition include chapters on crock-pot and freezer cooking, it is also Marjorie's first, reluctant attempt at writing recipes in metric:

[This book] has been the hardest, because of re-constructing the

BELT KNITTED FROM STOCKINGS IN MOSS STITCH

Cut stocking ¼ inch in width. With No. 11 needles, cast on 1. Increase each end of every row until there are 15 stitches, in moss stitch. Do two rows.
Next row: Knit 6, cast off 3, knit six.
Next row: Knit 6, cast on 3, knit six. Continue until belt is 27 ins. long, then decrease one stitch each end until there are none left. Cover a curtain ring with scallop stitch, then insert the end (without hole) through the ring and stitch down. Cover a button and place on the point where you stitched it. Cover another button and sew it on the other end of the belt about 3½ ins. from the point. When wearing the belt, push the other pointed end through the other half of ring and put button through the hole. I do not waste much in this household. It was drummed into me at an early age not to waste, to make do, or do without if you can't pay cash for it.

"Just as around your body,
This little belt you wear,
So may your life be circled
By 'heaps' of loving care."

recipes, etc. I did not want metric myself, nor did any of the older folk I have spoken with, but the younger fry couldn't use a recipe with lbs. and ozs., so I just had to compromise. So, for days on end I weighed from flour to mustard and milk to vinegar, etc., into cups and spoons from the amount on my scales, and in the measuring jug. It was tedious, frustrating and nerve-racking—one job I don't want to repeat.

The book's frontispiece is graced by a cosy honeymoon shot of Marjorie and Eric, and although Eric's presence does not infiltrate the third edition of the cookbook as pervasively as Adrian's does the second, there were substitutions: for example, Adrian's Scones were out, and Eric's Scones (a completely different recipe) were in. The poetry section is somewhat shorter, with the second edition's maudlin verses about love and grief excised in favour of material that is generally less personal. Marjorie has included diagrams of the sign language alphabet and introduced new prose sections on the nature of girlhood and boyhood. 'What is a boy?' is answered along the lines of 'as vigorous as an elephant, as soft as butter, as stubborn as a mule, and as lovable as Cupid', while 'What is a girl?' provides that the ideal is 'as delicate as a butterfly, as dainty as a flower, as cute as a princess, as cuddly as a kitten, as exasperating as the last page missing from a best story book, an angel in disguise'.

Marjorie's next publishing project was her most ambitious to date: an autobiography. *Life Is for Living: The Heartaches and Happiness of Marjorie Bligh: With Snippets of Travel, Wisdom and History* is a solid hardback volume with a bright blue dust jacket featuring images of Marjorie as a baby, as a young wife and as the book's 69-year-old author. Launched at Madden Street on Marjorie and Eric's tenth

ICE-CREAM BUCKET COVERED IN BREAD WRAPS

Great for storing or carrying small cakes or scones. Cover for a 5 litre ice-cream bucket and lid. Crocheted from bread wraps. It requires 16 bread wraps for bucket and 4 for the lid. One bread wrap crochets about 3 rows on the upper part of the bucket. Cut ½ inch wide, dust with talcum powder. Start with 6 chain. Join. Do 12 dc in the ring.

1st row: 2 dc in each dc.
2nd row: 1 dc in each dc. Repeat first two rows.
5th row: 1 dc in each dc. Repeat last row.
7th row: 6 dc, 2 dc in next. Repeat all round.
8th row: 1 dc in each dc.
9th row: 5 dc, 2 dc in next. Repeat all round.
10th row: 4 dc, 2 dc in next. Repeat all round.
11th row: 1 dc in each dc.
12th row: 3 dc, 2 dc in next. Repeat all round.
13th row: 1 dc in each dc.
14th row: Repeat last row twice.
16th row: Dc 10, miss 1 dc. Repeat to end. This should fit the bottom of the bucket. Now continue without increasing or decreasing until it fits over the bucket – about 33 rows.

LID

Do 6 chain. Join. Do 12 dc in the ring.
1st row: 2 dc in every dc.
2nd row: 1 dc in every dc.
3rd row: 1 dc, 2 dc in next. Repeat all round.
4th row: 5 dc, 2 dc in next. Repeat all round. Repeat last round 3 more times.
8th row: 4 dc, 2 dc in next. Repeat all round. Repeat last row twice more.
11th row: 1 dc in each dc.
Repeat last row 3 times.
15th row: 3 dc, 2 dc in next. Repeat all round.
16th row: 1 dc in each dc.
17th row: Repeat last round. This should now fit the top of the lid. Punch holes around the top of the bucket and in the hollow of the lid (next to edge). Sew on covers with a length of the cut bread wrap, using a running or back stitch.

Newspaper Logs

Fill a tub with cold water, add ¾ cup dishwashing liquid. (This tubful will do an awful lot of logs.) Mix well. Roll newspaper into logs – about two newspapers placed together and rolled tightly should do for each log. Tie each one with a piece of string each end. Soak logs in tub for about 24 hours. Remove and place in sun to dry. They take several days to dry. Make sure they are properly dry before using or they won't burn properly.

DYE LOT IN WOOLS: If it is necessary to use a different dye lot, leave sufficient to work two rows, then work four rows – two with the new dye lot, two with the old – then continue with new dye lot and any difference in the dye lots will be less obvious.

Knob Lost in Knitting

If you lose the knob off your knitting needle, glue the toothpaste cap onto the end of it.

Sticky Tape

If you cannot find the end of the sticky tape, hold it over a steaming kettle and the end will loosen.

Marjorie outside her local bookshop promoting Life Is for Living, *her 1986 autobiography.*

wedding anniversary, *Life Is for Living* is not for the fainthearted. It contains in excess of 250,000 words—more than four times the total word count of this book—in its 431 pages of small and closely packed type. Chapter headings include 'My Two Sons Gerald and Ross (both conceived on my birthday)', 'Prizes I Have Won in Shows and Competitions', 'Stories, Photos, Etc., That Have Made the Press', and 'Lies, Deceit That Led to Good Riddance'. At the beginning of each chapter, and scattered throughout the body of the text, are italicised quotations that are by turns funny, solemn and elusive (*'Rich foods are like destiny—they too shape our ends'*; *'Idleness rusts the mind'*; *'The calmest wives make the stormiest husbands'*). Dropped in wherever it strikes Marjorie's fancy, the quotations are an epigrammatic commentary on the events of the narrative.

The early chapters of the book are based on Marjorie's memories and written in a lively style, whereas the later chapters are based on her daily diaries and travel journals, and are consequently marked by rapid shifts between subjects and the inclusion of copious minutiae. In recording so much about everything Marjorie has created a remarkable time capsule of quotidian detail. An idea of the density of the text in the later chapters can be gained from the opening paragraph of 'Chapter 37: Our Canadian–American Holiday':

> Early January, our friend Tony Boghman was back in hospital with the second heart attack (and died on the 14th February). We called to see him (and another dear friend, Mrs. Pinner, who was to have an operation) on our way to Ross where we were going to celebrate my son Ross's birthday on the 20th, but Mrs. Pinner passed away before we returned home. When we arrived home Freda Fi Fi had to go to the vet as she had a grass seed in her vagina. Having it removed cost $19.50.

Marjorie lays no claim to literary distinction. In her foreword she cautions readers:

> I am a novice at writing a book and only attended a State School, but because I call a spade a spade, I'll be as frank as I know how in relating my good and bad experiences. I will try to tell you as much as I can without losing my dignity, as in one chapter I deal with divorce.

The final eight chapters of *Life Is for Living* offer blow-by-blow descriptions of the many overseas holidays the Blighs enjoyed after Eric's retirement from bus driving. Once Eric had sold his house and made the decision that he 'owed the world nothing' he put the proceeds of the sale towards travelling the world with his new bride. He and Marjorie saw parts of North America, Europe, the Middle East, Russia, China, Japan, India and New Zealand. The chapters in which Marjorie records everything about these trips, down to what she wore, the names of most tour guides and how much everything cost, have been known to best even the most devoted of her readers: 'We played Scrabble, looked at films—"Porridge" and "A Fine Romance"—snoozed, read and gorged, and were at Heathrow airport at 10 a.m. on the 26th (27th in Australia) . . . A bus took us to Victoria Station for $1.70 (Aus.) then we took a taxi to the

Telephone Book
Paste a suitably sized calendar inside your telephone book. Saves many trips away from the telephone to verify a date; saves minutes.

Telephone Calls (S.T.D.) [long-distance]
Set the timer on your stove when you are going to make an S.T.D. call, then you will know when to cease.

Telephone Tip
If you haven't an outside bell for when you are working in the garden, put the phone into a tin such as a biscuit tin, and you'll be sure to hear it then.

Vacuum Cleaner Bag Hints
Put a mothball into the bag, or spray with disinfectant to eliminate the stale smell of cigarette ash, etc., in the bag.

Put a cupful of used tea leaves into the bag and shake well. The dust clings to the leaves. Empty before vacuuming, then if you spill any, you can clean it up as you go.

If you run out of the standard bags for your vacuum cleaner, you can use the ordinary bags in which groceries come from the supermarket. Fitted carefully, these bags are strong and very suitable, as well as being free.

Make your own by using three thicknesses of old nylon curtains (not the lacy type). The suction is better, too.

Marjorie, Freda Fi Fi and Eric at Madden Street in the late 1970s.

Grosvenor Hotel that cost another $2.00 (Aus.) and our friend met us in the foyer.'

Perhaps the highlight of these years of 'overseas gallivanting' came in 1980, when Marjorie had the opportunity to present a copy of one of her books at Buckingham Palace to the Queen's private secretary, William Heseltine. Heseltine put Marjorie and Eric at ease by telling them he was an Australian and a former employee of Sir Robert Menzies, whose portrait Marjorie was pleased to see hanging in one of the palace's studies. Heseltine apologised that the Queen was too busy to meet with Marjorie (Her Majesty was getting ready to leave for Australia), but accepted both a copy of *At Home with Marjorie Bligh* on her behalf and a promise from Marjorie that she would send a copy of the same to Mrs Heseltine for her recipe book collection.

Life Is for Living is all the more remarkable when you consider that Marjorie wrote it by hand, twice. When she first took her manuscript to Alan Richmond, the man who would edit and print it for her, he said he regretted that her handwritten lines were much too close together—and sent her home with a fresh ream of paper, so that she could begin again with wider spacing. 'Sometimes I couldn't sleep as I never thought I would finish it, and my thumb on my right hand was aching, stiff, and nearly paralysed,' she writes, 'but once I start a project I will not give in.'

———

Two years after the publication of the autobiography came Australia's Bicentennial year, an important one for Marjorie Bligh. Though she is not untroubled by the impact of colonisation on Aboriginal people, she did not attach any disquiet to the pomp and ceremony that attended January 26, 1988. Rather, she woke up on that Australia Day with a huge sense of excitement. Even if Eric preferred to spend the day carting wood, Marjorie planned to sit down in front of the television to watch (and video tape) all the celebrations.

In 1988 Marjorie was keeping her daily journal in a special Bicentenary Pictorial Diary. She was also absorbed in the preparations for her own gift to the nation: a new book. Departing from her usual domestic territory, this was to be a book of history and facts into which she could pour some of the leftover detail she had researched while writing her autobiography. Titled *Tasmania and Beyond*, the book would be released later in 1988 as an 'Endorsed Bicentennial Project', and would earn Marjorie a Bicentennial medal. On the book's patriotic green and gold cover is a small cameo picture of Marjorie above a green map of the island state. In the bottom corners are green maps of the 'Western Hemisphere or New World' and the 'Eastern Hemisphere or Old World', and between these are the words 'Happy Birthday Australia, from Marjorie Bligh'.

Marjorie gave the book her customary personal touch. To illustrate the 'Convicts' section she included a photograph of her own convict forebear, her great-grandfather Henry Nailer. The World War I section is illustrated with a picture of Alf Martin, Marjorie's war veteran uncle. Elsewhere, Marjorie has included photographs of herself and her sisters, and the poodle Freda Fi Fi is pictured perched perilously on a sign at Cradle Mountain's Post Office Tree.

In 'Chapter 3: Achievers, Transport, Media, Etc.', Marjorie provides her own who's who of success and fame. In the course of sixty-six pages of potted biographies she notes important world citizens, ranging from Nostradamus to Kylie Minogue, from Dame Agatha Christie to Dame Enid Lyons, from Marie Curie to the Singing Kettles, a vocal and instrumental group hailing from the northern Tasmanian timber town of Scottsdale. She also includes a partially accurate biography of her own colossal fan Barry Humphries. A reviewer of *Tasmania and Beyond* noted that Marjorie, 'as if divining' that she

Night Light
On your way out at night, leave a torch in the letterbox, so when you come home you can light up the steps and path.

Bathroom Curtains
Bathroom curtains are better made of towelling, as they absorb some of the steam. Make them to match your towel set.

Ping-pong Ball
If accidentally crushed while playing, restore by putting it into a saucepan of boiling water for a few minutes.

Deodorant: Dab underarms with bicarbonate of soda and cotton wool ball. It is aluminium free.

sometimes strays from the path of precision, 'throws in one of her inimitable quotes: *"One should always aim at being interesting rather than exact."'*

'I look at these hands,' Marjorie said recently, 'and I just can't believe all the things they have done.' Indeed, in the waking hours of her ninety-four years those hands have rarely been still. In her diaries Marjorie carefully records her sustained and daily industriousness. If she has not been cooking or gardening, she has been scrapbooking or writing, or otherwise she has been knitting, sewing or crocheting. The sheer volume of handmade goods on show in her upstairs museum at Madden Street—aprons, dancing gowns, toys, bags, bookmarks, rugs, bedspreads, cushions, slippers, dressing gowns, hats and toilet roll holders—should impress upon any visitor just how seriously Marjorie has taken to heart the maxim 'As every thread of gold is valuable, so is every moment of time'.

> **WASH WATER (for hands):**
> Keep a large ice-cream container of hot, soapy water on the sink when cooking. It is handy for rinsing hands, or utensils; saves water too.

The museum was constructed in 1992, when Marjorie received an unexpected lump-sum payment of Adrian Cooper's superannuation entitlements. It seems that Marjorie decided just as soon as the cheque arrived how she was going to spend it. It's less clear, however, what the original purpose of the museum was. When the space was officially opened, on Marjorie's seventy-fifth birthday, there was press coverage of the event: one report suggests that the museum was built as a memorial to Adrian Cooper, while another suggests that

In 1982, as Marjorie's writing enterprises began to boom, she published her first gardening manual.

(from) **HOUSE PLANT HINTS**

* Put your plants under the shower now and then to wash off dust.
* To polish foliage and keep plants in good condition, wash leaves with 1 teaspoon white oil diluted in 1 cup of warm water. Use cotton wool to apply.
* Always use clay pots for indoor plants as they ensure plenty of evaporation and prevent soil from becoming water-logged. Also, painted flower pots cause injury to plants.
* The problem of loose stakes in pots can be overcome by screwing a piece of dowelling to a tin lid. Stand this in the bottom of the pot and fill with soil, the weight of which will hold the lid firm. Drill extra holes in the lid for drainage.
* Used tea bags make good drainage for a pot plant, saves finding pebbles and also acts as a reservoir.
* When going away on holiday fill a bucket of water and group your plants around it. Tear an old sheet into as many strips as you have plants and immerse one end of the strip in the bucket and tuck the other end in the soil of each pot. The moisture seeping down the material into the soil will keep your plants happy for a fortnight or so.

WHAT IS A GARDEN?

What is a garden?
Goodness knows!
You've got a garden,
I suppose:

To one it is a piece of ground,
For which some gravel must be found.
To some, those seeds that must be sown,
To some a lawn that must be mown.

To some a ton of Tassy rocks
To some it means a window-box;
To some, who dare not pick a flower –
A man for a dollar or two an hour.

To some, it is a silly jest
About the latest garden pest;
To some, a haven where they find
Forgetfulness and peace of mind . . .

What is a garden?
Large or small,
'Tis just a garden,
After all.

it was constructed primarily to contain the overflow of Marjorie's craft output and of Eric's bottle collection. Today, though it smells of must and mothballs, the museum is a site of homage for Marjorie's fans, and the pages of the large-format visitors' book are still being filled with expressions of amazement.

Preserved there are such treasures as a knitted 'story' bedspread that dates from Marjorie's years in Redpa. On each large square is knitted, or embroidered, a complex motif. On one square two blue love-struck budgies are captioned 'Marjorie and Adrian', while another features a pale grey map of Tasmania. Marjorie and Adrian's caravan is towed across one knitted square, and there are squares for various of Marjorie's beloved pets. More astonishing even than the amount of knitting that went into the bedspread is that Marjorie completed it in only a few months—proof that in her heyday she was an ace needlewoman. Also in the museum is a quilt from leftover scraps of fabric, the making of which Marjorie describes in her autobiography:

> Early March [1978] I started a quilt that took me 2½ months, or 228 hours. First, I cut out 1,368 rounds of different scrap material, using a saucer as a guide, felled the edges, then gathered each into a small rosette resembling a miniature shower cap. I then sewed one to the other—four joins on one rosette.

The fabrics are delicate and the handiwork superb; though the finished item may not be to everyone's taste, it is beyond doubt that it is beautifully made.

Shower Caps to Cover Food
When on holiday, you tend to collect a lot of shower caps. Don't throw them away as they are useful to cover bowls of food in the refrigerator.

The more notorious of Marjorie's recycled goods are also displayed in her museum. There are hats, table covers, vests, slippers and toys crafted from the thick, spongy, stretchy fabric that results from cutting up old pantyhose, spiral-fashion, and knitting or crocheting the long strips as if they were yarn. Marjorie's pantyhose items are—as you might expect—mostly in shades of beige, though some are alleviated by the occasional contrasting stripe of white, navy or bottle green. And it's not only her own that Marjorie has recycled. Once word was on the street, people would bring her bags of their old pantyhose. Likewise, they would bring men's ties that she would convert into aprons or cushion covers, and endless bread wraps and plastic bags that she would painstakingly cut up and crochet into rugs, hats, bags and coverings for discarded plastic containers such as ice-cream buckets, detergent bottles, soft-drink bottles and potato-chip cylinders.

When Marjorie was a child she was required to turn old materials into new goods because the new goods were genuinely required. But as goods became more affordable and quantities of waste skyrocketed,

SOAP FROM SCRAPS: Save all the pieces of soap and when you have a lot, melt them in a double boiler with a little water (or grate them first). Remove from stove when liquid and add some olive oil; stir and beat well. Pour into a pie dish to set. When cold, cut into squares and leave to harden. A beautiful beauty soap and as it floats it is a boon when bathing children.

RUG FROM WASTE

If you have children, you have from time to time sweaters, cardigans and even woollen socks that have become too small for them. Don't burn them but make them into a useful rug for the shack, car or bunk. All you have to do is cut squares from the best parts and sew them all together, then bind the edges. I have had several of them in my time, and I used to herringbone the seams for neatness, but now [that] I have a machine that does fancy stitching I do the edges with that. Of course, you have all the squares the one size. About eight inches square I generally use.

her mother's sensible ethos—waste not, want not—morphed into a
new credo. In her latter years Marjorie has turned old materials into
new goods not because those goods are needed, but because she feels
the need to do something—anything—with all that waste. A bread-

Marjorie created this bedspread by preparing and joining more than thirteen hundred rosettes of remnant fabric. The curtains, in 'crazy patchwork', were made from fabric left over from Marjorie's dancing frocks.

bag cover for an ice-cream bucket was, in her mind, both pleasantly decorative and a better alternative to the two bits of packaging being thrown into the trash. Marjorie would probably be surprised to know that her waste-recycling crafts have been lauded as modernist artistic practice in the pages of *Kritikos*, an 'international and interdisciplinary journal of postmodern cultural sound, text and image'.

Marjorie's enthusiasm for recycling was nearly the focus of a musical comedy in the mid-1990s. So taken was a Burnie-born playwright with Marjorie's long-standing commitment to reusing re-sources that he proposed a show with the working title 'When Life Hands You Lemons, Make Lemonade'. The playwright intended to cast his actress wife in the role of Marjorie, and himself in the role of a spiritual medium who contacts Adrian Cooper. Sadly for us

Toys knitted from oddments of yarn and used pantyhose.

all, the script was abandoned before the musical reached the stage.

Though Marjorie intended *Tasmania and Beyond* to be her last book (other than revised editions of her old works), she found herself under friendly pressure to publish on the subject of craft and recycling. Her 1995 volume *Crafts: Old—New—Recycled* is a triumphant meeting of form and content, its patterns themselves recycled out of the reams of magazine patterns that Marjorie has clipped over the decades. Perhaps the most splendid aspect of the book is its colour plates, which feature Marjorie and Eric modelling some of her more remarkable creations. Marjorie is seen in a red and gold short-sleeved sweater featuring the symbols for her and Eric's star signs (Aries and Taurus), and also in a pale-blue lacy bed jacket perfect for her favourite luxury, breakfast in bed. Eric is shown patiently modelling a range of knitted vests, as well as a matching tweedy-green cardigan, cap and glove set.

GLAD WRAP HINT: Glad Wrap is easier to handle and not so sticky if you keep it in the refrigerator.

Contact Lens

If you drop one, make the room dark, then shine a torch over the floor and the lens will sparkle in the light.

Coat Hanger from Bread Wrappers

Cut 4 bread wrappings into 20mm strips. Cast on 12 stitches with number 7 knitting needles and knit a strip the length of a coat hanger, then sew the edges together over the hanger. Makes a very pretty gift. Keep hands, needles, and bread wrap dusted with talcum for smooth knitting.

Carpet (small article lost)

To find a small object dropped on the carpet, pull a stocking over the vacuum cleaner hose, fasten securely and sweep over the area. The cleaner will suck the object into the stocking.

Christmas Wrapping Paper

Used paper can be made good again by spraying with spray starch and ironing with a warm iron.

Brassiere Renewed

A Mrs Dorothy Redburn of Burnie, who was 74 in 1986, sent me a sketch of a pair of bras she renovated, and asked me to pass the idea on. She said she cut away all the perished elastic at the back, and sewed on in its place some heavy duty elastic bandage that she once used for a sprained muscle on her leg. She now just slips the brassiere over her head like you would your frock.

Between 1981 and 1998 Marjorie produced five new books and five revised editions, her efforts culminating in her final publication, the fourth and most comprehensive edition of *At Home with Marjorie Bligh*. Weighing in at 668 pages, it brings together a lifetime of endeavour. 'This is my final book because I have written it under extreme difficulty,' Marjorie writes in her foreword, before going on to explain the vicissitudes she suffered as a result of a blocked tear duct.

Perhaps the fruitfulness of the late phase of Marjorie's life was due to the steady stream of praise and accolades that she received at this time, the memorabilia from which clutter the walls of her living room and fill the pages of her scrapbooks. Or perhaps the secret of Marjorie's success in this period was the companionship of Eric Bligh. His presence meant she did not suffer any bouts of debilitating loneliness, and he neither kept her from her work by causing her distress nor diverted her with the demands of high passion.

If not an especially romantic affair, Marjorie and Eric's relationship seems to have been a serviceable arrangement. There were times when they drove each other to distraction, and a long period when they slept in separate beds due to snoring. But, up until Eric's death, Marjorie regarded him with fond affection.

Suffering a stroke in April 1999, Eric went first to hospital and later to a nursing home, where he died in late December of the same year. By then, Marjorie was eighty-two and beyond any desire to seek out husband number four.

Pins (in rhyme)

"Pins are most elusive things,
So very apt to stray,
Keep them near when cutting out,
This very simple way;
Sew a little cushion to a firm elastic band,
Wear it like a bracelet,
And they'll always be on hand."

In recent years Marjorie has been forced by degenerating eyesight to give up many of her craft-based hobbies. But nothing can keep her from her garden, or from the sharp interest she continues to take in filling regular mail orders for her many books. Still looking after herself at Madden Street, with help from her regular visitors, 94-year-old Marjorie is described as well as ever by the motto pinned up by her oven: 'I was not born to be idle. I am like oil on the stove. I have to do something or I will explode.'

GLADIOLUS (glad-e-o-lus)

Gladiolus is derived from gladius meaning a sword, referring to the sword-like foliage. Gladiolus is a gross feeder. When you use liquid manure and you think "this will kill the lot", they have just had enough as long as you water heavy after.

To prepare soil for planting use a mixture of sulphate of potash, blood and bone and superphosphate on the basis of 2:3:4. This should be forked into the soil which has already been dug over to a depth of one spit.

. . .

Gladiolus take from 90–100 days to bloom from planting. If you plant corms in the first week in January, they will bloom in April, thus escaping the worst heat and thrips, but to do this, you will have to hold the corms reasonably dormant by keeping them in the refrigerator. If you want them to flower for Christmas plant in the middle of September. I always put mine in in July or August to escape the thrip.

. . .

Gladioli blooms were highly regarded during the Art Deco period. During World War II in Germany gladioli, said to be rich in vitamin C, was made into soup as part of the war-time diet.

Put gladioli bulbs for four hours in Lysol before planting (1½ teaspoons to 4 gallons of water).

5

The Edna Question

IN one of the aphorisms sprinkled like sugar through the pages of her books, Marjorie tells us: 'Gossip is when you hear something you like, about somebody you don't.' Though it's a handy quip, it's only half correct. Hearing something delicious about anybody will usually suffice, and enough people have liked the idea that an eccentric Tasmanian housewife was the inspiration for Barry Humphries' housewife gigastar, Dame Edna Everage, that a whisper to that effect has been in circulation for three decades.

At first glance it's plausible that Marjorie Blackwell/Cooper/Bligh was the blueprint for Australia's most famous domestic goddess. After all, Marjorie and Edna have much in common, even beyond the flamboyant glasses that Marjorie favoured in the 1970s and that Edna has transformed into an icon in their own right. Housewives, mothers and public figures, the two women have always been hugely ambitious, though neither of them pursued adulation outside the home in earnest until their children had grown up and left the nest. Each of them has long seen for herself an important role in educating the public about how to live. In print, on radio and—in Edna's case—on television and stage, they have dispensed their indispensable advice on cooking, cleaning, home decoration, fashion, beauty, etiquette, gardening, culture and history. Has anyone, even Isabella Beeton, ever claimed such breadth of expertise as have Marjorie and Edna?

Both present to the world a persona forged from a formidable alloy of sweetness and steel; it would be as great a mistake to underestimate Marjorie's will as it would be to trivialise Edna's wit. As public commentators they are each other's equal in their willingness to discuss the intimate details of their lives, and others'. Marjorie is every bit as forthright about her weak bowels as Edna is about her husband's prostate problems. Perhaps this frankness stems from the sure and steady self-regard both Marjorie and Edna have enjoyed throughout their careers, which has also driven both of them to memorialise their lives and achievements. While Edna's costumes and memorabilia are housed at Melbourne's Arts Centre,

In 1992 an unexpected windfall enabled Marjorie to commission the second-storey extension at Madden Street.

Barry Humphries

Barry Humphries was born on 17th February, **1934**, in South-East Asia, but brought up in Camberwell, Victoria. Barry is a comic genius conservative clown, actor, elegant writer and landscape artist. His first stage comedy appearance in a Melbourne University student revue in the early '50s was entitled "Call me Madman", and he played a variety of roles. His third wife Diane Millstead, 35, gave birth to their first baby, a son named Oscar Valentine, in 1981. Barry has spent most of his life in London since 1959, he has a mansion flat behind the Albert Hall in Kensington. Off stage, he potters about around Portugal, paints in Italy, and wanders through old European cities. Before the birth of 'Dame Edna Everage', housewife super-star, he had to beat a drinking problem and a nervous breakdown, but now he couldn't be happier with the man behind 'Dame Edna' and 'Sir Les Patterson'. Barry Humphries has recently been cast in wax as a model for sightseers to wonder at, at Madame Tussaud's in London. (Barry has all my books. As soon as I launch a new one, he sends for it – sometimes for several.)

—from *Tasmania and Beyond*

Marjorie's treasures are for the meantime carefully preserved in her home museum, where they will remain until her death, when they will be bequeathed to Launceston's Queen Victoria Museum and Art Gallery.

When I set out to uncover the truth about a connection between Marjorie and Edna, it seemed that the rumour was going to be quickly and easily quashed. First, the character of Mrs Edna Everage debuted in 1955, a decade before Marjorie came to public notice with the release of her first book. And then there was the testimony of Barry Humphries' extremely well-informed biographer Anne Pender, who describes Edna as an amalgam of influences including Humphries' aunts, his mother's friends, the CWA matrons Humphries encountered on road trips through regional Victoria and even Humphries' father, who was known for the catchphrase 'Hello, possums.' But then I discovered something that enabled me to keep faith that somewhere, embedded in the rumour, was a kernel of truth. The discovery came in a dowdy Hobart op-shop, within the hardback covers and hot-pink, gold-embossed dust jacket of Dame Edna Everage's 1989 autobiography, *My Gorgeous Life*.

Curtain Rods

Slip a finger from an old glove over rod for easy threading of lace curtains.

Nose Dry on Hot Day

Apply roll-on antiperspirant to bridge of nose and your spectacles won't slide down.

Beginning with an account of little mauve-haired Edna's discovery of her convict heritage, this tome encompasses its heroine's youthful brush with undercover Nazis, her marriage to Norm Everage, the abduction of her first-born by a rogue koala, the birth of her surviving children (Bruce, Valmai and Kenny), her billeting of a foreign athlete during the 1956 Melbourne Olympic Games, and her renunciation of obscurity, swiftly followed by her rise to international stardom. In the closing chapters Edna saves the Queen's day by ducking over to Buckingham Palace to run up a spectacularly successful passionfruit pavlova to feed to a party of Australian dignitaries. The first mention of pavlova is accompanied by an asterisk that points to an appendix of recipes and hints. And any combination of the terms 'pavlova', 'hint' and 'recipe', I knew, could lead deep into Marjorie territory.

Perishables Forgotten

Have you ever left your perishables in a friend's refrigerator after visiting on your way home from shopping? Solve the problem by putting your keys in the refrigerator too.

I forked out four dollars, and rushed home to compare Edna's and Marjorie's recipes and hints for the most iconic of Australian desserts. I turned first to *At Home with Marjorie Cooper*, which contains no fewer than eight pavlova recipes: Classic Pavlova, Stored-Heat Pavlova, One-Egg Pavlova, Kim's Pavlova, Marshmallow Pavlova, Easy Two-Egg Pavlova, Adrian's Favourite Pavlova and Delicious No-Bake Pavlova. But, to my dismay, wherever Edna found her generous six-egg-white recipe it was not in the pages of *At Home with Marjorie Cooper*, where the maximum number used in any recipe was four. Not even the list of ingredients in Edna's pavlova was replicated in any of Marjorie's recipes. Yet in Edna's appendix, underneath her pavlova recipe, there was a paragraph of useful tips on turning out the perfect pav. Compare her few lines, published in 1989:

> Always have the eggs at room temperature, and several days old. New eggs have thin whites, and will not beat up to great volume. A pinch of cream of tartar or a few drops of lemon juice strengthens the protein in the whites, giving it a strong structure.

with this excerpt from Marjorie's pavlova tips, published in 1973:

> Use eggs that are a few days old. If you use fresh eggs, the whites are thin and do not beat up to a great volume. They should be at room temperature before beating. Add a pinch of cream of tartar or a few drops of acid (lemon juice or vinegar) to egg-whites; this strengthens the proteins in the whites, giving a stronger structure and more volume.

It wasn't much, just a fragment, but it was something.

Putting aside *At Home with Marjorie Cooper*, I turned to its successor, the 1982 volume *At Home with Marjorie Bligh*. A nine-year interval—and a new surname—had given Marjorie pause to revise her pavlova offerings (Adrian's Favourite was among those scratched).

Though the later edition of the book still contained eight recipes, four were new: Pavlova (Australia's Own), Pavlova (Perfect), Pavlova (Lemon-cream) and . . . bingo! Pavlova (Friends). The pavlova of friendship—a big-hearted six-egg-white mixture—was the one that Dame Edna whipped up for Her Majesty Queen Elizabeth II in the kitchens of Buckingham Palace. Like any self-respecting cook, Edna had put her own spin on Marjorie's recipe, slightly adjusting the ratio of ingredients (more sugar, less cornflour), but other than slight changes to syntax the two recipes' methods were the same. It was enough to bring the Marjorie–Edna rumour back from the brink, and make it worthy of proper examination.

Like most people, I cannot tell you precisely when or how I first heard the rumour of a Marjorie–Edna connection. Most likely, I read about it somewhere. Or somebody told me. For once I had set out on a quest to answer the Edna question, I learned that 'I read about it somewhere' and 'somebody told me' would be the rabbit holes into which the rumour would disappear whenever I tried to pin it down. People who had told me with great certainty about the Marjorie–Edna connection became vague when I asked for specifics, and when I began to collect newspaper and magazine clippings concerning the Edna question I discovered that journalists had been consistently cautious in their phrasing.

Gates from Wagon Wheels
Your handy man can soon convert a pair into interesting double gates for your drive.

'Is it true?' I asked Marjorie over a cup of tea at the Madden Street dining table. 'Did you inspire Edna?'

'Well,' she said, 'I don't know about *that*.'

As I pressed further it became apparent that,

Marjorie in the private museum that houses Eric's bottle collection and other treasures alongside Marjorie's toby jugs, souvenir spoons, scrapbooks, dancing gowns, craft items and more.

as far as Marjorie is concerned, the relationship between herself, Edna and Barry Humphries is one of mutual admiration. For her part, Marjorie has kept a watchful eye on Barry's personal life and public career, keeping clippings in her scrapbooks about his various marriages and about Edna's stellar achievements. For his part, Barry has since the 1970s been Marjorie's most high-profile customer, ordering multiple copies of her books. And though the two have corresponded, and spoken on the telephone, they have never met in person.

'He invited me, once, to a show he was putting on in Launceston,' Marjorie told me. 'But I had a meeting that night, of the Devonport Friendship Club. I was either the treasurer or the secretary, I can't remember—so I didn't go. But I wish I had. It's one of my greatest regrets.'

According to her diaries and autobiography, Marjorie's first contact with Barry Humphries came indirectly, in November 1974, when Humphries contacted the printer of her book *At Home with Marjorie Cooper* (published in 1973) with an order for two copies. The following year saw Edna's star rising over London's Shaftesbury Avenue, as the theatre producer Michael White took on Humphries and launched his late-night comedy show *Housewife Superstar!* (the title was a humorous nod to *Jesus Christ Superstar*, which was playing just down the road). Marjorie's books clearly made an impression. When Humphries brought Edna home to Australia from England to perform in 1979, and his touring itinerary brought him to Launceston, he made an effort to contact Marjorie. Part of the publicity campaign was an interview on a northern Tasmanian radio station, during which he made a public appeal for Marjorie to ring in and speak with him. In *Life Is for Living*, Marjorie reports:

A lady rang on the 11th of September and said that Barry Humphries was asking after me over 7EX radio in Launceston, so

IDEAS FROM SUGAR BAG

Gay cushion covers can be made from dyed sugar bags, which wear well and look most attractive. They can be made in a jiffy by cutting two exact squares, then draw threads on each side for 1½ inches to make a fringe all round. Sew up three sides (on the right side near the fringe), insert a cushion to fit and then sew up the opening. A design can be worked on the corner if desired. I have Mr and Mrs pair. They look well in the sunroom, sewing room or verandah.

A soiled linen bag can be made from a dyed sugar bag also. Embroider "Soiled Linen" in bold letters, then put a zip fastener right along the opening. That is now the bottom of the bag. Insert a coat hanger through other end by making a small hole for the hook to pass through and shaping the bag to fit the hanger. The zip at the bottom enables you to get the soiled clothes in seconds.

I rang the station and Barry invited me to have dinner with him and be his guest at his show during the week. But I had to decline as Eric and I intended to resign from the Friendship Club the same evening because we'd had enough of the hypocrisy. Also in September I knitted Glenn a pair of gloves, Uncle Alf a scarf and myself a brown woollen cape and peaked cap to match.

Her diary entry for September 11, 1979, reads:

Eric went to Spreyton to get apples. I unpicked a bed jacket & made a pillow case. Dressed Freda's sores. Barry Humphries ask for me over 7EX. Miss Hine rang & told me. I rang 7EX & spoke to him. He ask me to dinner and his show.

It's not clear from either of these accounts whether Marjorie spoke with Humphries on air, or whether their conversation was conducted privately. If their exchange was broadcast, it might well have begun the Marjorie–Edna rumour.

In the early 1980s Barry Humphries snapped up the new third edition of Marjorie's first book, now titled *At Home with Marjorie Bligh*, as well as her *Homely Hints on Everything*. It seems he was sufficiently impressed with the books to give them as gifts to his friends. In *Life Is for Living*, Marjorie writes:

On the 7th July [1983] I received a letter, with an Australian $10 in it, and a request from Barry Humphries' children's nanny in England to send one of my books to Lady Craigmyle, 18 The Boltons, London. She mentioned that she often uses my book that Barry bought from me, and because she thought it excellent she wanted one for her friend. But because Barry had bought two of my books—the 'hint' one as well as the 'cook' book—I wrote back airmail and asked her which one. After several weeks of awaiting a reply, I wrote direct to Lady Craigmyle, and she did not have the courtesy to answer either. Early this year [1986] I gave the letter to our Post Master to see what he could do about tracing her. He had no luck either, and I still have not heard anything. I also wrote to the *Australian Women's Weekly* and they passed my letter on to Barry when he was in Australia. Also in July I cut the legs of 92 pantyhose into strips and knitted a man's pullover with some and crocheted the rest into 10cm squares to fashion into a table cover when I had enough done; and more stockings were given to me. I used up the tops by knitting them into slippers.

When the *Tasmanian Mail* reported on the autobiography in late 1986, journalist Martin Stevenson focused on the Humphries connection. He reported that a 'thrice-married Devonport author who numbers Barry Humphries and Max Gillies among her avid fans has just seen her fourth, and she claims last, volume through the presses near her Devonport home'. After a decade of occasional appearances in the press, the Marjorie–Edna connection was reported in *Who* magazine in 1996, as well as in a spread in the inaugural issue of the Tasmanian lifestyle magazine *40° South*. Across two pages ran a bold headline that asked 'Was Marjorie the Original Dame Edna?' In the text beneath the only answer provided is: 'Many Tasmanians believe she is the original Dame Edna. In a photograph taken at her wedding to her third husband Eric in 1976, the resemblance, especially the trademark cats-eye glasses, is astonishing.'

The Tasmanian photographer Paul County, who created the image used for the cover of this book, photographed Marjorie in 2003 when he was making a series of portraits of Tasmanian food identities. He placed Marjorie, then in her mid-eighties, against the backdrop of a retro kitchen complete with black and white linoleum floor, bakelite canisters and a curvaceous fridge. In her arms was a bouquet of gladioli. An exquisitely kitsch kitchen, a spray of gladdies and before your eyes . . . is Edna Everage.

'The photo was taken in a little museum in Salamanca Square. It was called something like Timewarp House, and when I saw it I knew it was perfect for Marjorie,' County said.

MAORI BISCUITS

These biscuits are eggless, keep well, and are made in a jiffy.

¼ lb. butter, 4 tablespoons sugar, 2 tablespoons of water, 1 cup of chopped dates, ½ cup walnuts (crushed), 1 heaped cup S.R. flour, 1 dessertspoon cocoa.

Melt butter and sugar over low heat, stirring well. Add water, dates, nuts, and flour in which the cocoa has been mixed. Put small pieces on a buttered tray and bake in moderate oven for 12 minutes. Can be joined together when cold with butter icing. Makes 5 dozen.

ANZACS (Biscuits)

Melt ¼ lb. butter and 1 tablespoon golden syrup, add 2 tablespoons boiling water in which has been dissolved a teaspoon carb. soda. Sift 1 cup flour with ¼ teaspoon salt, add 1 cup each of coconut, sugar and rolled oats. Mix into a stiff dough with the butter mixture, add a few drops of vanilla. Put into small lumps on a greased tray. Prick and cook in a slow to moderate oven until pale brown. Leave on tray for a minute before lifting off on to a cooler.

BRANDY SNAPS

Melt 3 oz. butter, 3 oz. golden syrup and 3½ oz. castor sugar. Sift 3½ oz. flour, pinch salt and 1 teaspoon ground ginger, add the grated rind of one lemon and the butter mixture. Drop in small lumps on a tray, leaving plenty of room for spreading. Bake 10 minutes in moderate oven. While still hot, roll into a lily shape around the handle of a greased wooden spoon. Push smaller ends through the square holes of a cake cooler to get cold.

PINEAPPLE CHANTILLY

3 dessertspoons gelatine, 4 tablespoons hot water, 6 slices Swiss roll, 2 or 3 dessertspoons sweet sherry, ½ teaspoon vanilla, 2 eggs, 2¾ cups milk, 1½ tablespoons arrowroot, 3 oz. sugar, 1 tin pineapple, 5 tablespoons coconut.

Dissolve gelatine in the hot water in a vessel standing in a pot of hot water. Place slices of Swiss roll in serving dish. Sprinkle over the sherry. Mix the sugar and arrowroot with a little of the milk; add the rest, then stir over heat until it boils 3 minutes, slowly. Cool slightly, then add vanilla, beaten egg yolks, dissolved gelatine, chopped pineapple and coconut. Fold in stiffly beaten whites. Pour into lined cake dish and chill until set. Decorate with a slice of pineapple and cherries. Serve with cream. Serves 6 people.

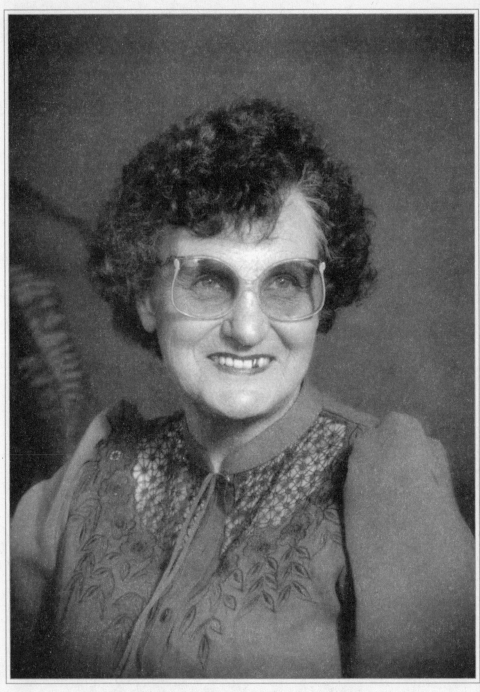

The style of glasses Marjorie favoured during the 1970s and '80s sparked comparisons to Australia's most famous domestic goddess, Dame Edna Everage.

In order to pose for County, Marjorie made the four-hour bus ride from Devonport to Hobart. She is fond of County, whom she coquettishly calls 'my boy in the south'. (One Christmas, he was touched to receive from Marjorie a recycled Christmas card, along with a bookmark knitted out of old pantyhose.)

A Swarm of B's

B hopeful, B happy, B cheerful, B kind,
B busy of body, B modest of mind,
B earnest, B truthful, B firm and B good
B sure your B haviour B all that it should.

B sharp in the morning, and never B flat.
B ware most of all that you never B that.
Be all of these things and whatever B fall,
B sure you'll be happy and B loved By us all!

'I bought the flowers for her as a way of saying thank you for coming,' County said. 'My original idea for the photograph was to have her standing at that stove, holding some kind of produce, but then I put the gladdies in her arms and it just looked so right. Of course, I didn't say anything to her about the Dame Edna connection. It was just my own little joke to myself, and something that other people might pick up on if they're interested in that sort of thing.'

But how did he first hear about the Edna connection?

'Oh, I don't really know. Probably somebody told me.'

———◦◦◦———

Clearly, the person I needed to speak to was Barry Humphries. I phoned and emailed his agent, his publisher, and various theatres and theatre companies, but was not reciprocally plagued with responses. Months passed, but I kept faith with the Edna question, and continued to search out any hints and echoes that conceivably connected Marjorie to Edna. It occurred to me that Number 32 Humoresque Street, Moonee Ponds—which achieved its pinnacle of stylishness in

THE PERFECT PAVLOVA (or Classic Meringue)

Named for a famous ballerina, the Pavlova can be temperamental at times. Here are a few tips that will help you make a perfect Pavlova.

Bowls and beaters must be scrupulously clean; the slightest trace of water or grease will prevent whites whisking stiffly. Carefully remove any trace of broken yolk, small pieces of eggshell, etc., before beating. Prepare oven tray before beating egg-whites, which will collapse if not used immediately. If you are not using quilted aluminium foil, brush oven tray with oil; other fats will solidify as meringue cools and make it difficult to remove it from tray. Use eggs that are a few days old. If you use fresh eggs, the whites are thin and do not beat up to great volume. They should be at room temperature before beating. Add a pinch of cream of tartar or a few drops of acid (lemon juice or vinegar) to egg-whites; this strengthens the proteins in the whites, giving a stronger structure and more volume. Egg-whites must be really stiff before you add sugar (in methods where whites are beaten first), otherwise the meringue will not be firm enough to support the sugar and mixture will not hold a firm peak. Beat whites until bubbly, add cream of tartar, and beat again until whites are stiff (if cream of tartar is in recipe). In some recipes castor sugar is used for quick dissolving; for others, granulated sugar gives a firmer result. Add sugar, a dessertspoon at a time, and beat after each addition until sugar is completely dissolved. Make sure that all sugar is dissolved, otherwise the undissolved sugar will melt during cooking and give a 'weepy' sticky Pavlova.

Where sugar is added gradually, make sure each addition of sugar is dissolved before any more sugar is added, otherwise the weight of undissolved sugar will break down egg-white aeration and mixture will collapse. When sugar is dissolved, the foam will be satin-smooth and glossy. To test if sugar is dissolved rub a little of the mixture between two fingers. Lift beaters from basin; the white that adheres to them should stand in stiff peaks. If peaks bend over, continue beating. Cornflour prevents sugar 'weeping' and helps dry out Pavlova; the more cornflour used, the drier will be the Pavlova. The combination of vinegar and lemon juice helps to form the marshmallowy centre; also whiten the Pavlova. Use cool oven (unless stated otherwise) to just dry out, not cook, and then leave in oven until cold.

1956—might bear more than a passing resemblance to Marjorie's dream home, Climar, completed in time for Marjorie to move in on Empire Day 1955. And so I spoke to Tim Fisher, the curator of *Ednaville*, the exhibition that reconstructed Edna's 1956 abode within the walls of Melbourne's Arts Centre (where Barry Humphries is the patron of an impressive Performing Arts Collection).

Tim Fisher explained how, when the idea for *Ednaville* was originally settled upon, Dame Edna published an open letter in the *Herald Sun*, asking for the 'return' of her original 1950s furnishings. Nearly a hundred people responded to the call, and Fisher spent weeks visiting homes all over Melbourne, delving into people's attics and sheds to uncover all the perfect period pieces that eventually furnished *Ednaville*. Fisher described how Humphries led the process of compiling the list of items required, and how specific he was about the colours, makes and models of the furnishings and appliances that communicated the essence of 1950s kitsch.

'Nineteen fifty-six was an important year for Australia. It was the year of the Melbourne Olympics, and Australia was opening out with the end of the White Australia policy,' Fisher said. 'It was the time when the housewife was really assuming the role of homemaker; an aspirational time.'

Au gratin (or-grar-tan)
Bisque (bisk)
Bechamel (Beshamel)
Bolognese (bol-on-asee)
Bouillon (Boo-yawn)
Cafe au Lait (Kafay-o-lay)
Canape (can-a-pay)
Chantilly (shahnte-yi)
Coq Au Vin (cock-ovan)
Croquettes (craw-kets)
Croutes (Kroots)
Croutons (Kroo-tawns)
Entree (on-tray)
Frappe (fra-pay)
Gateau (ga-toe)
Goulash (goo-lash)
Parfait (par-fay)
Piquant (pee-kant)
Puree (pure-ay)
Ragout (Ra-goo)
Ravioli (ra-vee-o-lee)
Saute (so-tay)
Souffle (soo-flay)
Vol-au-vent (vol-o-vahn)
Wiener Schnitzel (veener-schnit-zel)

Like Climar, *Ednaville* rep-
resented the pinnacle of mid-
1950s aspirational decorating
panache. Where Marjorie chose
sandblasted glass wading birds
for her entranceway statement,
Edna plumped for a wrought-iron
lyrebird security door for her street
frontage, and kept the sandblasted
reindeer glass for an interior
door that joined the sitting room
and the kitchen. While Edna's
sitting-room decor had a stronger
commitment to Australiana than
Marjorie's, the two women's
kitchens were remarkably similar.
But my investigation yielded no
hard evidence, only pleasing
similarities.

FIRESIDE STOOL

Make a fireside stool from
treacle or golden syrup tins and
a dyed sugar bag. You can make
a small one with three tins, or a
larger one with seven tins.

Cover each tin separately by
cutting 2 circles ¾ inch larger
than the top of tin. Measure
around the tin next, and cut
pieces of bag 12¾ inches and
4 inches (the size around a
treacle tin). Sew up the short
sides, sew one circle in, easing it
slightly. Turn inside out. Put tin
inside having the top of the tin
at the opening.

Place some cotton wool or
waste on the top of the tin, place
on the other circle and hand-sew
it to bag casing around tin, first
turning in the edges.

I put the Edna question on ice and turned my attention to other
matters. But then an email arrived, and the moment I read its subject
line I knew that I was back in the hunt. Although it was not addressed
exclusively to me, I felt that it was in some mysterious way a response
to the entreaties I had posted out into the world. The email was from
a local bookshop, telling me that Barry Humphries was coming to
Hobart to perform at the Theatre Royal as part of the promotion
for his new memoir, *Handling Edna*. I snatched up the phone and
called the bookshop owner, who in turn called the publicist who
was handling Barry Humphries, who in turn called the man himself.
Within a day it was arranged. I would meet Humphries at the Theatre

Royal prior to his show, and have a few moments with him to pose the question.

⸻ ⸳⸲⸳ ⸻

The Theatre Royal is the country's oldest theatre, and what it lacks in size it makes up for in its insistence on its own history and dramatic atmosphere. The cheap seats were once the domain of manacled convicts, and in more recent history such luminaries as Laurence Olivier and Vivien Leigh have graced the stage. There are plush carpets and upholstery in positively regal shades, gilt-edged mirrors, a frescoed dome above the auditorium and a gilt Cupid in the centre of the proscenium arch. Arriving in the foyer I chatted with the booksellers, who were loading trestle tables with mountainous stacks of the tell-all book Humphries was there to promote. It was a handsome hardback edition, and the pinks, purples and sparkles of its dust jacket were of a piece with the theatre itself. The scene was set, and into it, finally, swept Barry Humphries himself.

Attending to Humphries was a publicist from his publishing house, an elegantly dressed woman with an air of fearsome efficiency underpinned by her neat English accent. She introduced me to Barry and stated my business. There in the foyer, still draped in his overcoat and shadowed by his hat, he began to talk about Marjorie. He spoke quickly, his words coming out in perfect sound-bites that might almost have been rehearsed.

'And that's really all I can tell you,' Humphries said, turning away as if I were dismissed.

But I'd not had my tape recorder running, I protested, and I had quite a lot of other questions. I was permitted to follow, upstairs to the Dress Circle foyer, where everything had been prepared for Humphries to sign a towering stack of *Handling Edna* copies. Humphries' voice records just as it sounds in person—rich, textured, practised. He answered my questions, and asked questions of his own, and although the book signing meant that I did not have his full attention, the percentage that I did have seemed genuinely engaged. I was grateful that he was able to repeat the comments that he had made in the downstairs foyer, and with embellishment. But his thoughts trailed off each time we were interrupted—by the theatre manager, wishing to be introduced; by Humphries' phone ringing (someone from London, reminding him that it was the birthday of one of his relatives).

At one point I brought out the article from *40° South*: the one with the headline that asks 'Was Marjorie the Original Dame Edna?'

'What's this?' Humphries asked, eyes scanning, face delighted. 'Why have I never seen this?'

I asked him if he had read Marjorie's autobiography, and as I pulled it out of my bag he stopped signing books and took it from me.

'I had no idea she had written an autobiography. Why haven't I got this? Read to me from it!' he commanded, with pleasant imperiousness, as he handed it back.

I found myself, like everyone around him, doing his bidding and reading out some of the more salacious highlights of *Life Is for Living* instead of using the precious time to get answers to my questions. And yet I did manage to learn this much:

'Edna,' Humphries said, 'was an existing person before I ever stumbled across Marjorie Bligh, but I did on a visit to Australia get hold of her book and realise it was a treasure trove. I immediately bought several copies and gave them to friends, mostly in London. Some were bound in a rather fragile manner . . . so I had some rebound with proper hardbacks and I corresponded with her and

Marjorie with souvenirs from one of the many overseas holidays she enjoyed with her third husband, Eric.

I've even spoken to her on the phone, but I have never physically met her. I think at first she came to be pleased at my communications. I did write to her quite a few times.

'What struck me was that she seemed to be a much more accomplished Edna. The appearance, something about the smile. There was a kind of—dare I say it?—relentlessness about the smile. It was also voracious. Voracious.'

But, I wanted to know, did Marjorie inspire Edna, even though Edna was an existing character? Was it possible that Edna used Marjorie's books as reference books when she needed a recipe, or some hints for how to turn out a perfect pavlova, for example?

'Oh yes, Edna refers to [Marjorie's books]. I've cooked things, she's cooked things, from Marjorie's books. And stains. It's very good for stains.

'I've used her poems, even reprinted some of them, I think in Edna's biography. And some of her sayings. I've probably pirated them, without permission. There was just a wonderful affinity, and I was only sorry that more people on the mainland didn't know what a genius lived down here. This is a Renaissance woman. Knitting, darning, stain removal, cooking, gardening and, of course, no slouch in the matrimonial department. The only thing Marjorie couldn't do was perform. She wasn't an actress.'

Could he remember exactly how he learned of Marjorie?

Jar Lid Removed

Removing a tight-fitting screw top jar can be exasperating. Try gripping the lid with a piece of sandpaper – the lid should unscrew easily now.

'As I said, I came upon her book when I was in Australia,' he said, as if that were the last word on the matter. 'You must send her Edna's best wishes, or mine. I'll sign a book for her . . . how do you spell "incomparable"?'

Without so much as smoothing away a

frond of her sleek black fringe, Humphries' publicist rapped out I-N-C-O-M-P-A-R-A-B-L-E with British-boarding-school precision and at a perfect pace for Humphries to inscribe the frontispiece with a sparkling mauve message for the incomparable Marjorie. He handed me the book, making me promise to deliver it with his and Edna's fondest wishes. My audience with Barry Humphries was over.

Humphries had mentioned that Brian Thomson—the stage and screen designer whose many claims to fame include the flamboyance of *The Adventures of Priscilla, Queen of the Desert*—also admired Marjorie. Over the phone from his home in Sydney, Thomson reminisced about his admiration for Marjorie, which began in 1970s London, where he and his brother Ken were part of a creative coterie of expatriate Australians. Thomson had originally gone to London as the designer for the smash hit *Jesus Christ Superstar,* and came up with the title of *Housewife Superstar* for Edna's star vehicle. He even appears in photographs as Edna's beloved youngest son, Kenny.

POSSUMS (Discouraged)

Discourage possums from gobbling buds and leaves with quassia solution. Quassia chips are obtainable from the chemist. It is very bitter when made up with water. Boil 125g (4 oz.) in 4.5 litres of water for two hours. Dilute the yellow liquid when cool with five parts water and use as an all purpose spray around trees, or, crush a block of camphor, mix with petroleum jelly and smear on the trunks of trees. Renew after 3 weeks, or after heavy rain. Also, try planting a ring of chives around the trees. Best plan of course is an electric fence.

'Myself and a lot of English friends, we were very into Marjorie. We were all very into kitschy things at the time,' Thomson recalled. 'I'm not sure if I first got onto her through Barry or through my brother, who is a good friend of Barry's.'

Thomson told me how he referred to Marjorie's book in order to whip up a cake for Humphries, whose birthday took place during an impressive garbage-collection strike in London. 'The whole of the city was piled up with rubbish, so I made Barry a cake decorated with bags of rubbish and rats. I would have made the cake from a recipe in Marjorie's book,' he said.

'I found her books very useful, for practical purposes. I remember once, when a friend of mine had not dried his clothes properly, I went to her book to find out how to get that smell out. I thought she was much better than Mrs Beeton, because she spoke a language I understood. She's very no-nonsense.'

But as well as being a source of practical information, to this gang of homesick Australians Marjorie's books were also a rich source of nostalgia and hilarity. For them, Marjorie was a proponent of a

GIVE THAT OLD VASE A FACELIFT

If you have a vase that needs an uplift, or you have a nicely shaped bottle that is too good to throw out, why not make it into an attractive container for your flowers. Firstly, save your egg shells until you have about a dozen. Dry them in the sun, firstly taking off the skin that adheres to the inside. Paint the vase or bottle and while still wet sprinkle on the crushed egg shell until well covered. Let dry. Paint again and repeat the sprinkling of the egg shell. It gives a pleasing effect. In a vase I made are grasses I collected in the south of Tassie whilst caravanning once with my husband. I dyed them all different shades with food colouring and although they are several years old they haven't faded.

Marjorie models a handcrafted evening gown from the late 1970s.

particular kind of Australian identity: one that these Australians abroad could mock and celebrate.

'I think there's a lot of Marjorie in Edna,' Thomson confirmed. 'I was involved when Barry did his first coffee-table book—my brother was then the publisher at Harrap books—and it was rather fashioned after Marjorie's book. [Barry's] book went further in the Australianness of it all, but the homeliness was the same . . . For Edna, Marjorie's books would have been a goldmine.'

And a goldmine they were, especially when Humphries launched Edna's writing career with the *Dame Edna's Coffee Table Book: A Guide to Gracious Living and the Finer Things of Life by One of the First Ladies of World Theatre*. Like Marjorie's books, Edna's is wildly multifaceted, incorporating recipes, poetry, beauty hints and gardening wisdom, as well as advice on etiquette, napkin folding, pronunciation, art, history and travel. A number of the recipes in Edna's book are clearly based on Marjorie's, and in a later book—

"Flower Garden" from Coal

Fill a glass bowl with pieces of coal, about the size of very small apples. Mix in a separate bowl: three tablespoons of ammonia, two tablespoons of common salt, three tablespoons of cold water and some colouring. For colouring, use powdered prussian blue ink, or any one of the other powder colours. Food colouring is also quite satisfactory.

Pour the mixture over the coal and place the bowl in a very warm place, such as in front of a heater. In less than 24 hours the coal will begin to grow. The growth looks like the top of a cauliflower and can be maintained in different colours by mixing every other day one teaspoon of salt in one tablespoon of cold water with a little colouring. Carefully pour down the side of the bowl. At first it is very fragile but after a while the growth becomes crusty and is fairly durable.

Dame Edna's Bedside Companion—Edna bases her stain-removal hints on those compiled in *At Home with Marjorie Cooper*. But Humphries is not bashful, either about his debt to, or his regard for, Tasmania's most famous homemaker. 'I think there should be a Gideon Marjorie,' he told me. 'A copy of Marjorie's book should be in every hotel room. We've got to get Bligh-itis going. The things that woman made! Such unexpected constituents!

'I think Edna has never admired anybody as much as she admired Marjorie. I don't think she would have a bigger fan than me.'

MANY years ago when I was living at Campbell Town I was the town's dressmaker. I also organised balls and dances for charities, so, naturally I created many dazzling evening gowns for myself for those special evenings. One was of white lace with a full circular skirt. When it showed signs of wear I cut it into strips about 4 inches wide and oversewed the edges on the machine and made a lovely nightgown case. . . . In the centre I put a celluloid doll cut off at the waist. I made a frilly blouse of lace for it, and it graced my bed for many years. It's marvellous what you can do with left-overs and some deep thinking.

*This hand-knit in sparkly red yarn features symbols
of Marjorie's and Eric's star signs.*

Coda

I met Marjorie in 1995, when I was working as a journalist for Hobart's daily newspaper, the *Mercury*. In the dining room at Madden Street I took notes as she talked about a recently released book, *Crafts: Old—New—Recycled*, and about her career and principles. In my article I recorded that Marjorie told me she abhorred waste, and if I dropped dead at her table she'd have my body in her compost heap in a trice. Undaunted, I risked a turn around the garden with her husband Eric, and signed the visitors' book in the upstairs museum.

I can't say that Marjorie made a huge impression on me in our first meeting. Once I had converted my notes into a column of colourful fluff for the pages of the *Mercury*, I thought no more of her . . . until a few weeks after the article was published, when the paper's editor came thundering through the newsroom to my desk, steam pluming from his Scottish ears. He'd just had Marjorie on the phone, roasting him for my failure to clip the article and post it to her, after I'd promised her that I would. He passed the roasting on to me, with interest. I clipped the article, sent it to Marjorie—and never forgot her.

After that, Marjorie kept cropping up in my life. Just before I was married, I was given a copy of *At Home with Marjorie Bligh* (fourth edition) as a semi-ironic gift at a semi-ironic wedding shower. After my grandmother (herself a splendid filler of biscuit tins) died, my aunts let me have her cake tins and cookbooks; among them was a disintegrating copy of *At Home with Marjorie Cooper*. Soon I was seeing Marjorie everywhere—in magazines and newspapers, on television—her every appearance shadowed by the rumour about Dame Edna.

When I returned to Madden Street in 2007, to propose this book, I found the place little altered. Eric was no longer alive, but the house was still cluttered with piles of Marjorie's books; there were still sheaves of correspondence on the benches, and cushions on every chair, and doilies on every doily-able surface. While the abundant garden showed signs of getting out of control, it was still obviously loved.

From my previous experience with Marjorie, I knew that if I made any promises I would be held to them. If I embarked on the project of writing her story, there would be no question I would finish it. And indeed, she underlined these expectations over the top of the Anzac crumbs, when she passed me a folder in which she had filed the correspondence of all those who had gone before me, and failed. There was the play script that never quite made it, and a television documentary too. The letters showed how people began with high hopes, and ended up apologising.

At the time of my second visit Marjorie had just turned ninety, and the stakes were high for her. I left Madden Street understanding that she regarded me as the knight she was entrusting with her grail

There are cushions in the dining room
and also in the hall,
There are knitted toys and funny clowns
and pictures on the wall.
There are dresses in the wardrobe,
and evening bags in the drawer,
There are slippers galore that I'll never wear out
and by the look of my patterns there'll be more.
There's shopping bags made from plastic bags,
and baskets made from cane,
Beautiful hats from stockings,
They send my friends insane.
Lace doilies grace the table tops,
My bedspreads are fantastic,
There are so many different home made mats,
and even ones I've crocheted in plastic.
There's home made vases and jewellery,
and trunks full of knitted wear,
There's patchwork rugs and curtains,
That makes visitors stand and stare.
Aprons, bedsocks, scarves and hankies,
Tablecloths, suppercloths and more,
You'll find them all in my home,
From the ceiling to the floor.
I have no tiresome worries,
of gifts for Christmas Day,
as I make all kinds of present,
In my own particular way.
What is the secret of my skills
I am asked most every day,
I tell them perseverance and patience,
and the ability to pray,
as well as finish all you start,
Is one of my motto's too,
and if a thing's worth doing it's worth doing well
Is all applied to everything I do.

quest. And yet, other than stressing that she was counting on me to get the job done, Marjorie has taken a hands-off approach to this book, never once seeking to control, or even to influence, what I wrote about her.

Though I have spent hundreds of hours with her books and diaries, and talked with her, I still struggle to get a fix on Marjorie. At times, on the page, I have found her difficult to warm to. But while she is often self-serving in her explanations of past events, she is also honest enough to supply the facts that allow readers to construct alternative understandings. In person, I have always enjoyed her frankness, humour and generosity. But I have always known, too, that she would have me on toast in a flash if I vexed her or let her down. It has been difficult to reconcile the written Marjorie with the living one, and simultaneously to understand the multiple versions of Marjorie that have manifested during her ninety-four years.

What is certain is that in the marvellous, messy, unmediated avalanche of Marjorie's writings there is a little of everything. There is advice that is really very sensible, and advice that is clearly crazy. There are funny stories, mad stories, sad stories, stories that beggar belief. Marjorie has cast herself in every role, from schoolgirl to mother, wife to other woman, victim to victor, stepmother to wise woman.

Today, she is the grande dame of the housekeeping scene. From her home in Madden Street she diligently answers her daily correspondence, much of which now comes from a new generation of mothers and homemakers, young women turning to Marjorie for inspiration as they seek a new, frugal domestic ethic that is fit for a young and challenging century. Though mildly bewildered by the virtual world in which these women interact, she is deeply flattered by what they say about her on Facebook.

Perhaps, in the end, the most remarkable thing about Marjorie is her openness. By documenting her life so thoroughly, she has revealed every facet of herself and invited access to every fluctuation in her emotions and perspectives. Just as Climar and Mar-ian were always places where strangers were welcome, through her writings Marjorie has flung wide open the doors to her long, long life: a domestic life that has been at once remarkably ordinary and utterly extraordinary. A life that has, indeed, been for living.

We are all amateurs as we do
not live long enough to become
professionals.

I can go to my grave and say that
I have never been idle; I loathe it
so always find something to do.

My ultimate aim is to finalise all
the endless projects that occupy
my brain, or, even surpass them,
and I ask God to give me work
till my life shall end, and life till
my work is done.

BOOKS BY MARJORIE BLIGH

Marjorie Blackwell at Home (1965)

> *At Home with Marjorie Cooper* (second edition, 1973)

> *At Home with Marjorie Bligh* (third edition, 1982; fourth edition, 1998)

Marjorie Bligh's Homely Hints on Everything (1981; second edition, 1988; third edition, 1993)

A–Z of Gardening (1982; second edition, 1990)

Life Is for Living: The Heartaches and Happiness of Marjorie Bligh: With Snippets of Travel, Wisdom and History (1986)

Tasmania and Beyond (1988)

Crafts: Old—New—Recycled (1995)